FACING THE FIRE

GENEVIEVE MCKAY

STONEPONY STUDIOS

CHAPTER 1

BREE

There are moments in life when the whole world feels beautiful and enchanted. Like the air has an extra sweetness to it and everything you put your hand to miraculously turns out the way you want.

That's how it felt when I'd first come home from the hospital and began working with Lorne and the horses. Like my entire existence was charmed.

Before my time in the hospital, I would never in a million years have pictured myself working with horses and learning to ride any more than I would have taken up elephant herding or jumping out of a plane without a parachute.

But here I was, not only riding but working at a barn full time. And I was officially listed as one of the founders of our October Horse project. Our mission was to find new homes for retired racehorses.

I had even been given my own young thoroughbred, Ace, to

retrain. He wasn't exactly mine, but he was the next best thing to it.

I also ran a popular blog and a handful of social media pages for the farm. People loved hearing about the horses and my followers just kept growing at an exponential rate.

The entire autumn and early winter after I'd moved to the farm had been like a dream come true. I'd assumed it was sort of an apology from the universe for the year of painful dying that had come before it. And I'd somehow thought that my new charmed existence would go on forever.

But after Christmas, when the real winter set in, my idyllic life came to an abrupt freezing halt. Gone were the soft sunny fall days where the air was crisp and clear, and the horses had an excited prance to their steps.

Gone was the perfect winter vacation where Nicholas and I spent every day together, talking excitedly the whole time we worked about books, ideas, and the future. And finally, magically, stealing kisses when nobody else was around.

After the holidays, Nicholas had vanished back to school, barely bothering to text me let alone come home to visit. And the hard reality of working with horses during the coldest, most miserable months of the year kicked in.

The whole world became socked in with snow. Plows moved back and forth daily on the road below the farm, their blades grinding across the gravel as they pushed great drifts into the ditches.

The power went out constantly. Everything froze in a stubborn layer of cold. Ice had to be broken out of the buckets, the hoses seized up, and we had to make endless trips lugging water to make sure the horses had enough to drink. The gate latches had to be forced apart every single time or you had to stand there blowing your hot breath on them long enough to melt the frozen clips.

The path down to the barn had become a treacherous skating

rink that was dangerous to cross on foot or with a vehicle. Both Julie and I had skidded down it multiple times, but when Lorne slipped and fell coming out of his driveway, that was the final straw.

We'd had to call the ambulance when he couldn't get up, and they'd whooshed him away to the hospital to make sure nothing was broken. Luckily, his X-rays had turned out fine. He'd walked away with a bump on his head and a few bruises, but the experience had been enough to scare all of us badly.

Julie had had enough. She made a phone call and soon, a man showed up with an oversized dump truck full of sand. It took hours but eventually, the driveway and parking lots were coated in a thick brown layer of sand. It looked filthy against the white snow but at least gave us traction.

The ring was too deep and frozen to ride in and there were some days when it was too icy to even turn the horses out. Something they resented strongly. They were used to being outside all day in all sorts of weather, so they neighed and pawed, digging holes in their bedding. They paced and banged the doors impatiently with their hooves, demanding to be let out. They got bored of their hay nets and Dragon and Nipper found all sorts of inventive ways to rip theirs off the wall and stomp them

Even gentle Ace would sigh sadly while I brushed him, staring longingly at the rear door of the barn that led to the pasture. For him, even a snowy pasture without grass was better than being locked inside.

Chloe's project horse, Dragon, was awful to handle if she'd been cooped up for more than a day. Getting her back out to the pasture each time the ground thawed took two people and a lot of willpower. The second her lead rope was unclipped, she would take off to the far end of the field and not show her nose back at the barn until the last part of the day, long after the other horses had been tucked back inside.

"We need some smaller sand paddocks," Julie had complained,

shaking her head. "I hate to see them locked in their stalls without being able to stretch their legs."

I agreed with her when it came to the horses needing exercise, but I couldn't say the same about myself. I would have gladly stayed inside next to the woodstove until Spring. The frigid air outside hurt my lungs. And I had to constantly wear a scarf across my mouth and nose whenever I was outdoors. My muscles ached all the time and I was always freezing. Even with the woodstove crackling away non-stop, the big drafty farmhouse never seemed to get warm enough for my taste.

"Welcome to real farm life, Bree," Lorne had said when he'd overheard me complaining bitterly about the weather to Chloe. "It isn't all sunshine and trail rides. This is what separates the fair-weather riders from the real horse people."

"Yeah, yeah," I'd said ungratefully as I'd carted yet another water bucket past him.

Easy for him to say when he didn't have to carry buckets or push overflowing wheelbarrows of frozen poop-nuggets through the snow. His age, and his fall on the ice, had slowed him up quite a bit, and he'd taken a backseat on the physical work. But he still showed up at the barn each day to supervise. And he looked downright happy to be bossing us around while we worked.

"You can give it up anytime you like," he'd said casually, taking a sip from his coffee cup. "You don't have to stay if you don't want to."

I confess that for a moment I considered it. I pictured myself back in my warm bedroom at home working on … working on what? Living with my parents again? Going back to do university courses that hadn't meant anything at all to me? Never seeing the horses or my friends at the farm again?

"No, no," I'd said quickly, glancing over to where Ace was working on his hay net. "Of course I want to be here."

"That's what I thought." He'd given me a hearty pat on the

back that sloshed half the water out of the bucket and had walked away whistling way too cheerfully under his breath.

But there was another secret reason I was so frustrated about the weather. Despite the success of my remission, there was always the chance that I might get sick again. We didn't really know which of the drugs, treatments, or miracles had made me recover. I was still doing two drug trials and there was a part of me that was terrified that maybe one day the drugs, if they were even doing anything at all, would stop working. I was terrified of getting sick again.

I had so many things that I still wanted to accomplish in my life and each day that I wasn't actively working my way through my goal list felt like it had been wasted. Sometimes I could almost feel the hours ticking away.

I hadn't even sat on Ace yet. And I dreamed of exploring with him on the trails and cantering him effortlessly around the ring. I tried to hold that vision tight in my mind and tell myself that winter would be over soon, but it was getting harder and harder to convince myself.

"Just be patient," Julie kept telling me, "the weather will change, the racehorses will come and soon, you'll be riding Ace."

Julie had turned out to be much kinder and more sympathetic than I had originally thought when I'd moved in. I had not been sure at the beginning what sharing a house with Julie would be like, but it turned out that underneath her sometimes prickly exterior she was a comforting sort of person.

It was always nice to come back indoors where the woodstove was perpetually blazing, and she always had something nice baking in the oven or bits of tack spread across the kitchen table to be cleaned and oiled.

Still, sometimes even homemade cookies couldn't cheer me up.

"I don't know how we're ever supposed to train all the new horses in *this*," I said glumly on one extra dreary afternoon after chores were done. It was a slightly warmer day and the ground had thawed enough for Chloe to force me into the promise of an afternoon trail ride. But right then I wanted nothing more than to hide away inside.

I absently twisted the horse charm bracelet on my wrist. It had been a present from Lorne's wife Gretta before she'd died, and I never took it off.

I stared gloomily out the window at the rapidly falling snow. The entire hillside that sloped down to the barn was knee-deep again. Another layer piling up on the snow that had already fallen. "We can't even *see* the ring let alone ride in it."

"Oh, stop fussing." Julie laughed and set a chipped blue pottery mug of tea on the table in front of me. "You're worse than Lorne. The horses aren't even here yet. Who knows what the weather will be doing by the time they arrive? It could be balmy sunshine by then."

"I doubt it," I said, sighing heavily. "This looks like it's going to last forever."

"Of course it won't. Seasons always pass. Besides, Gretta usually liked to let the horses rest for a few weeks when they first arrived. It's nice to give them a little time to decompress when they come fresh off the track. We can work on their ground manners and give them some time to get used to their new surroundings."

"But we're getting paid to *train* them," I said stubbornly, wrapping my hands gratefully around the steaming mug. Despite the woodstove crackling away in the living room I was still cold. I was *always* cold. The illness that had nearly killed me last year had stripped my body of all of its fat reserves, leaving me pretty much unprotected in this unseasonable winter. Even wearing thermal socks and multiple layers of sweaters, I was nearly always shivering.

To be honest, I'd never really liked the winter, even when I was a kid. Other people liked to frolic in the snow and work up an outdoorsy sweat doing things like skiing and snowshoeing, but not me. I preferred to spend my winters hibernating with a blanket, hot chocolate, and a stack of books to read through. This apparently wasn't an option anymore now that I had a stable full of horses depending on me.

"Won't the board of directors think we're wasting their money or something by having the horses just sit there?"

"I doubt it." She shrugged. "It's all part of the process and it also happens to be out of our control since we're not in charge of the weather. Go on now, drink your tea so you can warm up and then go on out for your trail ride. Chloe is probably already down there waiting for you."

"I guess so." I sighed, eying the temperature gauge stuck to the outside of the window. Humans really hadn't evolved to be outside in weather like this. We would have been born with appropriately thick fur if that were the case.

"You don't want to ride?" Julie said, a flicker of concern moving across her face. "Are you doing okay? Do you feel sick? Is the work too much for you? Have you been taking your vitamins and minerals like you're supposed to? You might be low on vitamin D. A lot of people get the winter blues when they're—"

"No, no, I'm fine," I interrupted quickly, gulping my tea in an effort to finish so I could end the interrogation.

Honestly, she was worse than my own mom sometimes. Ever since I'd moved into the big farmhouse, it was like Julie had gone from being my aloof riding instructor to taking on the role of my protector.

"I mean, yes, I'm fine. I've got it all under control. The weather just has me in a bad mood, that's all. Working here is definitely not too much."

I looked away, escaping her piercing gaze. If I told her that I was tired and sore all the time she might say that the farm was too much for me. She might want to send me away. I couldn't risk that.

Although, now that I thought about it, I *might* not have been quite as good at taking my vitamins and supplements lately as I usually was. I took the drugs for the trial like clockwork but I sometimes slipped up on the other stuff. Maybe she had a point. It was pretty easy for me to become anemic if I didn't stay on top of things and I knew that could lead to low mood, loss of energy, and all sorts of random things.

I made a mental note to take something as soon as I was back from my trail ride.

"All right, as long as you're sure. I know I always say that a good rider rides in all types of weather, but that doesn't apply if it actually makes you sick. If it's just the cold that bothers you, then we should probably find you a pair of those fleece breeches that Chloe has. She doesn't seem to get cold."

That's because Chloe is practically superwoman, I thought grumpily and then pushed the uncharitable thought aside. Chloe was wonderful. She was a nice person and a brilliant rider, and she seemed to have an inexhaustible well of energy that never ran out.

Everyone loved her, including me, but I wasn't a good enough person not to feel the tiniest bit jealous at how perfect she was. And it wasn't my long stay at the hospital and near-death experience that made me weaker than Chloe, either. Even at my peak, I hadn't been even a quarter of the athlete that she was. She was small but mighty and she rode the feisty mare, Dragon, like a dream, even though the mare was a rank handful for most people.

"Here, make sure to take some cookies for the road," Julie said, setting a Tupperware full of fragrant biscuits in front of me. "They're from a packaged mix but I added nuts and chocolate so they taste like homemade. You need to keep your strength up."

"Thanks, Julie." I put my teacup in the sink, eager to escape before she launched into another lecture.

"And Bree …" she hesitated and then pushed the Tupperware

of cookies into my hands. "I hope you're not upset that Nicholas hasn't been around much. I know he cares about you but with his schoolwork load this year—"

"Of course not," I cut her off, forcing a smile and turning abruptly toward the living room. My boots were stored with the others on a mat right next to the crackling woodstove. "He's busy with school. That's fine. Totally fine. No big deal."

"I'm so glad you understand. I want him to enjoy this school year." She paused and then said the rest of the words in a rush. ""He didn't get to have much fun growing up. I was hurt so badly after the accident and I needed help with so many things. Even though I tried to give him a normal childhood, I don't think he ever stopped worrying about me. I was hoping that university would give him a chance to just let loose and have fun. But of course, he's taking it seriously, like he does everything. He always wants to give a hundred percent to anything he puts his mind to."

"I know. I think he's happy there, Julie. I'm glad he's having fun."

That part was true. But I wanted him to be having fun *here*. Which I knew was completely selfish of me. And I didn't want Nicholas to have to deal with the uncertainty of *my* future either. He deserved to be happy.

I stood as close as I could to the fire, letting the heat sink into my bones and waited until Julie moved back into the kitchen before letting the smile slip off my face.

Nicholas didn't owe me anything. We weren't even a couple. Not really. Kissing someone wasn't an eternal promise. A fact that I should have known better than anyone else. I'd practically moved in with my last boyfriend, Duncan, and he'd still managed to cheat on me with my sister when I was in the hospital.

I was sure the few kisses and deep conversations I'd shared with Nicholas probably meant way more to me than they had to him anyway.

He was at school surrounded by smart and beautiful girls all day long. Was it even fair for me to expect him to give up having a normal life for someone like me? Someone who might have a pending expiration date stamped on them that might be coming due at any moment.

I thought about his last text, sitting unanswered, on my phone.

Sorry, can't talk now. Busy helping a friend study.

That had been a week ago and I hadn't heard from him since.

I sighed, holding my hands out gratefully toward the heat. I glanced down at the thick rubber tray that had been set up beside the stove for drying boots and gloves. One half of it had been taken over by the fat black and white cat, Tom, who'd oozed himself into the space like a warm pudding.

"How do I get an uncomplicated life like yours?" I asked him, pushing gently at his jiggly body with my socked foot. He mewed sleepily, half-rolled over on his back and broke into a low purr, not even bothering to open his eyes.

I let myself stand there a few more seconds, inching as close as I could to the glass fireplace door without setting my breeches on fire, letting the warmth penetrate my bones.

At least my boots are pre-toasted, I thought, slipping on my posh new warm winter boots. They'd been a Christmas present from my parents and were thickly lined inside to keep my toes toasty, but they also had a heel so I could ride. I hadn't realized at the time that I'd be completely living in them for the next three months.

Gloved, hatted, and scarved, I grasped my Tupperware of cookies and headed outside into the biting cold. How on earth had Chloe convinced me to go on a trail ride on a day like this?

"It will just be a short one across the fields," she'd promised. "Dragon needs something to keep her mind occupied. Besides, we have to toughen you up."

She was right about that first part. Her project mare Dragon was a busy girl and if you didn't keep her engaged with something constructive to think about then she'd find ways to make your life completely miserable.

I slid down the long road to the barn, bypassing the sandy spots when it wasn't too steep so I could play on the ice a little. If you balanced yourself just right, it was a little like skiing. I slid slowly past Lorne's cozy cottage that had been built halfway between the barn and the big house on the hill. Smoke puffed cheerfully out of the chimney and I could just imagine him sitting in his easy chair by the fire with his coffee and his horse training books. It turned out that Lorne enjoyed winter about as much as I did and was using his advanced age as an excuse to stay tucked indoors as soon as he was done supervising our barn chores.

I didn't blame him one single bit.

CHAPTER 2

BREE

I finally made it—without falling—to the barn parking lot.

The front doors had been rolled back only a couple of feet in order to keep the wind from rushing through the aisle at full force. Even with the overhead lights on, it was dim inside, which made the stable seem a little shabby and run-down. I was suddenly worried that it wouldn't be fancy enough for the racehorses that were arriving in a couple of weeks. They were probably used to a lot more luxury.

"Hey, there you are," Chloe called from Dragon's stall. "I thought you'd bailed on our ride. I brought Nipper in for you already. I don't have too much time this afternoon. My mom has to work so I have to get home to babysit my brothers."

"Sorry, I'm here now," I said sighing. "But I really don't like—"

"The cold, I know," Chloe laughed. "You've told me like one million times. Now tack up that pony."

"You'd better eat some of these while they're warm," I said, handing the Tupperware of cookies over the stall door.

"Oooh, thanks. That almost makes up for you being late."

"Hey, Nipper," I said, rolling back his door.

Nipper popped his brown and white nose up from his pile of hay, gave me one look, and then dove back down again, shoveling food in as fast as he could.

"You just keep eating," I told him with a laugh. "I can brush you in here instead of the cross-ties. You might as well stay comfortable."

The Paint's lush russet and white coat had nearly doubled in thickness since the onset of this unusually bad winter. He looked like a velvety plush children's toy with his dark eyes and thick mane and tail. I ran the round curry comb through his woolly coat and then smoothed it all back down again with a softer brush. I rested my cheek against his sturdy shoulder for a second, inhaling the sweet smell of horse and hay.

"Are you excited about your new roommates?" I asked him, although of course there was no way he could know that he was about to get five new neighbours straight from California. Originally, the plan had been to just take in two racehorses, but somehow the number had swelled to five. "You're going to have to explain to them about all this snow, Nipper. They're probably going to go into shock when they find out how cold it is here."

"Are you talking to that horse?" Chloe said, setting Nipper's saddle and pad over my stall door with a thud and then placing the girth and bridle on top. She was clearly trying to speed me up as best she could. "He doesn't understand words, you know."

"Yeah, yeah. I like talking to him, though. And besides, you talk to Dragon all the time. I've heard you."

"I know." Chloe laughed. "But with Dragon it's good to just remind her that I'm there from time to time. Sometimes I think she forgets I'm even on her back when I'm riding."

"I believe that."

I had to take my gloves off to do up Nipper's girth since it was getting a little snug against his ample sides. Once it was done up, I took a second to slip my hands under his thick mane where the heat practically radiated off him. I closed my eyes in bliss and held them there to thaw for a minute.

"I hear all this talk about global warming," I muttered, "but I don't see it."

"Hot water?" Chloe said, appearing impatiently in front of me again. She held up a mug of steaming water that she'd poured from the kettle in the tack room.

"Sure, thanks." I grabbed Nipper's bridle and, folding the jointed snaffle in half, I submerged his bit in the water long enough for it to not feel like ice anymore. It was a routine that was annoying but necessary since the frozen metal bits would feel awful going into their sensitive mouths. I held the metal up to my cheek to make sure it wasn't too hot and then finished tacking Nipper up.

I had to admit that the world outside was beautiful, even though it was doing its best to kill me. The snow had stopped falling while we were tacking up and, like a miracle, the sun had come out. Although there were still dark, ominous clouds hovering over the mountains in the distance, the sky over our heads was a brilliant blue.

Nipper strode along with his ears pricked and his mane bobbing while Dragon did her usual sideways prancing and head tossing. Her steamy breath rose around her head in plumes that made it look like she was a real dragon about to breathe fire.

"She's full of it," Chloe said, laughing. She took one hand off the reins long enough to pat Dragon's rock-hard neck and was rewarded by a half-bolt that ended in a buck.

I couldn't in a million years understand why none of Dragon's behaviour scared Chloe. I wasn't the one riding the horse and nearly everything she did terrified me. Even the thought of ever getting on her back made me break out into a cold sweat.

Whenever the horse acted up, which was about seventy percent of the time, Chloe just sat there with a smile on her face like it wasn't happening.

It baffled me that nothing seemed to bother Chloe. I'd asked her a few times about how she could be so brave, but her answer was always just to stare at me in confusion like she didn't even know what I was talking about.

"You're just different people," Julie had told me when I'd admitted to her how much Dragon intimidated me. "You like a calmer, quieter horse and there's nothing wrong with that. If it makes you feel any better, I wouldn't enjoy riding Dragon much more than you would. She's a *lot* of horse."

The horses' hooves crunched through the snow in a satisfying way and despite the cold and my grumpy mood, I actually began to enjoy myself.

"Do you want to let them move out when we reach the field?" Chloe asked, her eyes gleaming with excitement. By *move out* she meant let Dragon gallop before the horse exploded. Her prancing hadn't slowed down in the slightest and she'd graduated to doing little hops of frustration with her front legs. Sort of a half-canter move that advanced her along like a manic rocking horse.

There weren't many places we could go faster than a trot because of the sketchy footing. But the neighbour's big open hay field behind the farm was full of soft drifts that wouldn't hurt the horses' legs or cause them to slip.

"Sure," I said with a sigh, knowing that Dragon would make the choice for us with or without my agreement.

Nipper caught her excitement when we reached the field. He made a little squealing noise under his breath and arched his neck, his ears pricked with excitement.

"Okay, okay but take it easy. You're not as young as Dragon."

"Ready?" Chloe said grinning.

When I nodded, Nipper and Dragon leapt forward at the same time, snow flying up in all directions. But about two milliseconds later it was just Nipper and I galloping along by ourselves while Dragon and Chloe disappeared somewhere in the far distance.

"Bye Chloe," I said, laughing a little. I wasn't sure what had made Dragon's old owners retire her from the track, but it couldn't have been lack of speed. I'd never seen a horse move as fast as she did.

Nipper's gallop started to slow into a relaxed, rhythmic canter and I eased the reins out so he could use his head and neck freely to navigate the drifty terrain. He snorted happily, and in a few minutes, we dropped into a trot and then finally a walk so he could have a breather.

I took the time to catch my breath too, filtering the cold air through the warmth of my scarf. My lungs were functioning much better than they had before, but they still got overwhelmed if I wasn't careful.

I looked around the big field with a sigh of contentment. It was impossible to stay unhappy when the sun was out and the snow around me sparkled like diamonds in all directions.

The terrain rose and fell softly here. We were in the valley that separated the hilly farms on the right from the long stretch of woods lower down on the left.

We weren't the only horse farm in the area. The whole long hillside was thick with horse properties of all shapes and sizes. Some large and fancy and slightly intimidating, some just cozy farms with two or three horses and one that had just a travel trailer, a three-sided shelter, and a small herd of miniature donkeys.

We wouldn't go that far today while there was snow on the ground, but I knew that at the top of the hill and off to the right was a proper posh eventing barn. It was complete with its own sprawling house, indoor arena, and a private cross-country course with professional looking jumps.

Chloe was dying to ride there but, unfortunately, we weren't allowed to use it. Julie had said that the family who owned it were nice enough, but they liked to keep to themselves and didn't want strangers traipsing all over their property. Which was too bad because that indoor arena would have come in mighty handy in the snow and the rain.

Only the top part of their property was fenced so anyone could ride the winding trail that ran halfway up the hillside and have access to all the trails and the woods beyond.

Directly down below them, in a rolling valley, was a small farm that was set up for horses but didn't seem to have them anymore. From the trail above, we could see a cozy brick house, a building that Lorne had said was a pottery studio, and a big greenhouse.

And, if you rode onwards past that, there was a small, tidy farm with a two-stall barn that was painted blue to match the house and a set of identical paddocks and a little pasture.

That farm also a full-sized outdoor dressage ring that was now buried under snow. Only two horses lived there; a shaggy senior pony and a massive dark bay with the most gorgeous, lush mane and tail I'd ever seen. His hair was always kept in tidy braids and he wore a blue tail bag in the rainy season to keep his magnificent tail free of mud and tangles.

His name was Thor, and Chloe always stopped to admire him and say how fabulous he was. She knew the owner a little since they had competed at some of the same shows, but she didn't seem to think overly much of her.

That was as far as I'd ever ventured on horseback, although Lorne had told me that it was possible to ride for days without running out of trails to follow. If, no *when*, summer ever returned, I was looking forward to doing more exploring.

"Not today though, Nipper," I said, reaching down to scratch his fluffy neck. "Just a circuit of this field and we'll head home."

Nipper was not at all worried at Dragon's disappearance. He strode along happily, his stride long and even and his ears pricked. We'd gone on so many trail rides with Dragon by now that he was completely used to being abandoned. She always turned up again eventually.

Sure enough, there they came over the far hill, now on the opposite side of the field heading back in our direction. They were down to a fast canter or maybe a slow gallop now. Even from this far away it was obvious that Dragon was in her element.

Chloe continued down the far fence line until she'd looped behind us and then I could hear her pounding up on the outside of Nipper, giving us plenty of space as she sailed by.

"One more loop," she called out breathlessly, "and then we'll come join you."

Her cheeks were flushed and her eyes were bright, and I thought that never had I seen anyone look happier or more alive.

We followed leisurely in her wake and I kept myself warm by doing walk, trot transitions, halting Nipper ever so often and asking him to back up a few steps just to keep his mind occupied.

We were strolling along on a loose rein by the time Chloe caught up with us again. This time when she asked Dragon to slow down the mare agreeably dropped into a walk beside us. Her sides were heaving, her nostrils were red and puffing, and there were faint patches of sweat on her neck and chest, but she looked like she'd had the best ride of her life.

"That's better, isn't it, girl?" Chloe said, gasping for air a little herself. She patted the mare's neck and allowed Dragon to walk on a completely loose rein. She turned to me and grinned. "This horse is going to be something, Bree. She's one in a million."

Thank goodness there's only one of her, I thought, suppressing a smile. But I had to admit that Dragon was both powerful and beautiful. Once Chloe could reliably channel all that crackling energy, they would be a team to be reckoned with.

We turned slowly for home, doing walk-jog transitions all the way back to stay warm and to keep the horses' muscles from seizing up.

"Car," Chloe said as we neared the barn and I looked up the hill with my heart suddenly thudding.

For a fleeting, exhilarating, second, I thought that maybe, just maybe it might be Nicholas coming home after all.

CHAPTER 3

BREE

*T*he car wasn't Nicholas's little green Volkswagen, though. Of course, it wasn't. It was a fancy-looking burgundy SUV that I didn't recognize parked just in front of the stable doors. We didn't get many visitors in the winter, or at least not in this awful weather, so I had no idea who it could be.

"It's a rental car," I said as we rode closer. "Do you think it's Jeremy-from-Scotland arriving early?"

Chloe drew in a quick breath and froze in the saddle, her gaze fixed on the car with a suddenly eager expression.

We had our first working student set to come live with us in a few weeks time, although he'd been a little vague about his exact arrival date. He was supposed to be some hotshot rider from overseas and he also happened to have large, soulful eyes, a chiselled jaw, and wore a permanently sultry expression. Chloe was a little obsessed with him and had been doing some heavy online stalking.

"No," she said, sighing heavily, "Jeremy-from-Scotland would never accept an SUV as his rental car. He'd drive a sports car or a hummer or something. Besides, we're supposed to pick him up, remember? I've already picked out my outfit. Maybe it's a board member. Maybe they want to bring the horses early."

"Well, I wish them luck with that. If they step off the trailer in this weather the horses will be begging to go back to California. "Oh no –" I broke off, seeing a familiar figure dressed in knee-high boots and some sort of furry overcoat waving at me frantically. "It's my sister."

"Angelika?" Chloe sent me a quizzical look. "Well, what's wrong with that? I thought you liked her now."

"You're right, I do," I said quickly, feeling a little guilty. Angelika and I were working hard to mend our strained relationship but that didn't mean that I was right-away thrilled to see her. That stab of mistrust was always there first. "She's just best served in small doses," I said with a rueful smile. "I wonder what she wants."

We could hear her calling my name excitedly before we were even halfway up the hill.

I sighed and then put on my polite, company face. If I was going to be the social media liaison of our October Horses project, then I had to get used to being professional in all sorts of situations. Even situations that involved my sister.

"Hi Chloe. Hi Bree, it's so good to see you," she squealed, coming down the path to meet us in her impractically heeled, and yet somehow beautiful, suede boots.

"Angelika, you'll get dirty," I said, eyeing up her gleaming white fur coat and matching hat. It looked real, but I knew that she was against using animal fur, so it was most likely an expensive fake.

It was seriously astonishing that someone who looked that good, like they'd just stepped off a runway in Paris or something, could be related to me. There was a sharp contrast between her in her bizarre, designer Nordic outfit and me in my second-hand breeches, thick boots, and battered barn jacket covered in dirt and loose bits of hay.

"Oh, I don't care about getting dirty. I love seeing the horses. I can't wait for Julie to teach me to ride this summer. Maybe I could ride one of our own racehorses."

"Er, maybe," I said slowly, but her genuine smile was contagious, and I ended up beaming back at her like a good sister. Which is what I should have done in the first place. It was hard to remember that we were friends now and not enemies. Old habits took a long time to die.

I jumped down off Nipper, gave him a pat, and then ran my stirrups up and loosened his girth. Beside me, Chloe hit the ground with a thud.

"I've got to grab Dragon's wool rug and then cool her out," she said smiling. "I'm already late and I'm supposed to be home to babysit my brothers in like twenty minutes. Good to see you again, Angelika."

"You too, Chloe."

"Come on, let's go in the barn where it's warmer," I told my sister. "Is Eddie here?"

"No, he's in LA still, but I had to fly into Vancouver anyway, so I thought I'd stop in and visit, and see Mom and Dad, too."

"Oh, yeah. How's that going?" My parent's relationship had been rocky for a while, but they'd taken to outright fighting for the last few months. The tension between them could be intense, and I think my sister and I both wished they could either just make up completely or get a divorce.

"Weird. Awkward. Mom spent the weekend desperately trying to pretend that everything was normal while Dad mostly hid in the basement working on his creepy little doll sets."

"They're not dolls," I said, laughing and rolling my eyes. "They are historically accurate dioramas. His work is kind of important, you know. He has museums all over the world calling—"

"Well, whatever, they're weird. I don't know why he can't work on happy stuff rather than all those battles and executions and things. Every time I go down there, all I see is war and beheadings. It's gross."

She had a point. Dad's models were sort of battle-heavy. But most of the events that historians considered important were unfortunately very war-like, so that's usually what he got asked to build.

"Anyway, I didn't come here to talk about our dysfunctional parents. I wanted to ask you a favour."

Ah, here it comes, I thought, all my senses suddenly on high alert.

"Oh, stop looking like that. I'm not asking you for a kidney. I just want to talk."

"I doubt you'd want my kidneys," I said, leading Nipper down the aisle and into his stall. His hooves clopped on the concrete in an easy, comfortable rhythm that instantly calmed me down. "They're probably half-shot."

Angelika made an exasperated sound under her breath.

"*Anyway*, you remember the Wilsons, right?" She leaned up against Nipper's stall door, watching my face expectantly while I took off his bridle.

"Umm." I wracked my brain. Were they neighbours, relatives, childhood friends?

"You know, they just came out with that song, Glide, that's on the local radio sometimes. They were semi-finalists in Canadian Talent a few years ago."

"Oh, they're *singers*. Right, I think I've heard of them then. Aren't they that weird hippy couple that has all the performing kids?"

From what I remembered, they were like a family of ten who

all had waist-long blonde hair, even the boys, wore flower crowns, and sang religious folk music or something. Not my cup of tea. At all.

"Yeah, I guess they were a little out there when they started out. But they've modernized, they have a proper manager now, and their music has become really popular. They actually have fantastic voices. They're about to do their first real tour this year so it's a big deal. And they're good people. They've been through a lot to get where they are."

"Okay, that's nice," I said slowly, wondering where this was heading.

"So, here's the thing. One of the kids, their daughter Adeline, had a bit of an incident on stage recently and now she can't sing for a while. She's not going to be able to go on tour with her family. They don't think it would be a good idea for her to go."

"They don't? Why not?"

"Well," Angelica looked away and I suddenly sensed that there was something she wasn't telling me. "It's a little complicated. They had a bit of bad luck last year; there was a house fire and some of the kids were trapped inside. Adeline was the one who got them all out, but she'd inhaled a lot of smoke and she had some damage to her throat."

Angelika broke off and I looked up to see her staring blankly at the back of Nipper's stall as if she were playing over some sort of scene in her head.

"She couldn't sing anymore?" I asked, wincing.

I could imagine that to a singer, losing their voice would be the worst kind of torture.

"No, she *can*," Angelika said slowly. "At least most of the time. But her voice changed. I actually think it sounds better, more interesting, than it did before but not everyone agrees. Their brand is being sort of sweet and light, and now here she is with this raw, bluesy voice. When she pushes herself too hard, it strains the vocal cords all over again. They had a bit of backlash when she started performing after the fire. Some fans don't like change."

"That's horrible."

"It's the nature of the business." Angelika shrugged. "You lose old fans; you gain new ones. Eventually, you develop a thick skin and stop caring so much what other people think. But that takes a while."

She sighed heavily and I wondered what sort of things had happened to make my sister develop her own thick skin. We'd never even talked about her life as a singer. I'd been at university and then in the hospital during the initial rise of her career and I'd missed most of it. It must have been hard for her to do all that on her own.

"Okay, and why are you telling me all this?"

"Well, the timing couldn't be worse. They are just about to go on months of touring, and nobody is sure what to do with her."

"She can't just go along with them and not sing?"

"Er, no," Angelika frowned. "At least, I really don't think that would be good for her. Her manager is a real…" she broke off again and frowned. "The thing is, Bree, I was hoping she could come here."

There was a loud expectant pause while I tried to take in what she was saying.

"Here?" The word came out sounding harsher than I meant and we both winced.

"She loves horses," Angelika said quickly. "They grew up with a pony and she knows how to ride. They lived on a farm in Kelowna up until the fire. Bree, she's still too young to be alone for all those months by herself and she's been through a lot. I think … I think she might be out of options. I know this would be a good, safe place for her to land."

"You're saying you want to drop some kid *here* for me to babysit while her parents are travelling around the world?"

"Er, just around North America. They're not *that* big a deal yet. And she's sixteen, so not a kid. And she's very independent. I bet you'd barely notice her here at all."

"Uh-huh. Well, I suppose I can ask Julie and Lorne, but I already know they're going to say she's too young. And she'd need to fill out an application—"

"Come on, Bree, can't you just make an exception on this one? She follows your blog and she loves horses. She's a good rider. I think she'd be a perfect fit."

She was looking at me so earnestly that I had to glance away. I fished a carrot out of my grooming tote and fed it to Nipper, listening to the steady crunch, crunch of his teeth while I tried to gather my thoughts. Angelika obviously cared about this girl for some reason, but I knew that she wasn't telling the whole story.

"Honestly, her parents don't have much money, but they *are* willing to pay for her to stay if you'd keep her here. It doesn't have to be a real working student position."

"It's not up to me, though."

"Please, Bree. She's a good kid who just needs a safe place to land. They're not sure what to do with her if she doesn't come here and they're actually quite worried about her. Her mom was even talking about the rest of the family not going on tour if they couldn't find her somewhere safe to stay. And that would set their career back years."

"I suppose …"

"And it would be so nice to have her in a place where someone is at least looking out for her. Someone who cares about people like you do. I could stop in to check on her whenever I was in town. Just say you'll think about it."

"Oh, for pity's sake," I said grumpily, "fine, whatever."

"Thank you," Angelika squealed, practically breaking the sound barrier. Nipper threw up his head and looked at her in astonishment before going back to eating.

Angelika threw herself on me and wrapped me in a tight hug.

"I didn't say it was going to happen," I said, extracting myself with difficulty. "I'll have to ask Julie and Lorne, and they might say that she's too young. We'd decided not to take anyone under the age of eighteen."

"She's mature for her age," Angelika said quickly. "I promise."

"Uh huh. Well, honestly, there is so much to do around here that we could use all the hands we can get. But if she's not going to work just as hard as the rest of us do then her parents will really have to pay board to make up for it."

"Yes, absolutely. Whatever you need. But she is a hard worker and she's honest and polite. You'll love her. I promise."

"Okay, I'm not sure how you know this girl. And I'm not sure why you care about this so much but, I'll see what I can do."

Angelika still hadn't left by the time I'd untacked Nipper, put his blanket on and turned him back out in the pasture. So, I couldn't exactly disappear to the warm house and leave her behind.

Right, I'm supposed to be polishing up those social skills, I thought, giving myself a mental kick. All I really wanted was to stand under a boiling hot shower for about an hour, get into my pajamas and spend the rest of the day cuddled up next to the woodstove. But it didn't look like any of those things were in my immediate future.

"Would you like to come up to the house for some hot chocolate and cookies?" I asked in my politest company voice.

"That would be great," she said eagerly, "let's drive my car up." Which, I had to admit, was much better than my expected return trek through the snow.

Lorne was already up at the house, going over one of our endless to-do lists with Julie. With five new horses coming in and the new working student set to arrive, our lives were about to get very, very busy.

"Angelika," Lorne said in delight, "it's good to see you. Come on in here and get warm. That is quite the outfit you have on."

For some reason, Lorne had a fascination with my sister and

her boyfriend Eddie. He watched them like they were an exotic city-dwelling animal exhibit at the zoo. He found Angelika's designer clothes, her ever-changing hair, and her jet-setting lifestyle to be like watching a reality TV show. He could never understand why Julie and I didn't feel the same way.

I was more reserved because I had a lifetime of mistrust built up between me and my sister. Something I was working hard to get over.

And Julie was picky about who she let into her life. She also knew the history of that epic last fight between Angelika and me. About how my sister had slept with my boyfriend when I was sick in the hospital. So, her protective instincts over me sort of kicked into overdrive when Angelika was around.

I'd noticed that she was slowly warming up to her, though.

"Come on in, let me hang up your, er, coat. Sit down and we'll get you a hot drink. You must be freezing."

They watched in fascination as Angelika sat down on the couch and began the process of unlacing her knee-high suede boots. Apparently, zippers weren't a thing in the city anymore. Too boring and too easy to use, I guessed.

Tom, the cat, even woke up from his perpetual sleep, stretched luxuriously and sauntered over to my sister, purring happily as he rubbed back and forth against her designer pant suit. Then he leapt into her lap, leaving a smear of black and white cat hair down her sleeve.

"You are just the handsomest," she told him, squishing her face into his fur. "If I didn't travel so much, I would definitely have a pet. Bree and I were never allowed to have animals growing up. I didn't even get to have fish until I was a teenager."

I remembered that. Angelika had plead for a dog non-stop for years before my parents had finally gotten her an aquarium with fish. Later on, she'd added another tank with a lonely hermit crab.

Why hadn't I helped her get us a dog? I wondered suddenly. I'd loved animals too, and I would have absolutely loved a dog in my life. But at the time, I'd pretended that I didn't want one just because it was something that Angelika cared about.

I sighed heavily, not incredibly happy with the direction my memories were going. It wasn't nice being the villain in someone else's story.

I'm going to have to help her rescue this kid of hers, aren't I? I thought in resignation. *I suppose I kind of owe it to her for being such a crappy older sister.*

Everyone made small talk and drank their hot chocolate while I sat nervously in the corner, suddenly wondering what they'd say when Angelika brought up the subject of the child singer she wanted to foist on us. Now that I was partially on board, I was worried that Lorne and Julie would just say no.

Apparently, I needn't have worried because they didn't blink an eye when she asked. They were clearly better people than I was.

"Oh, the poor thing. If you can vouch for her character then I'm sure we can make room for her," Julie said, instantly melting when Angelika told her the same story she'd told me. "The poor girl sounds like she's going through a lot."

"I can definitely vouch for her character. You'll love her. All the kids have been homeschooled so they're smart and mature. They speak a few different languages, too."

"We'll need more hands this spring for sure. And even if she can't ride, she can still clean stalls, help out around the house and do yard work," Lorne said, his eyes gleaming a little at the thought of more free labour.

"Absolutely, whatever you need," Angelika said, matching his smile with a Cheshire-cat-grin of her own. "There's just one tiny catch that I might have forgotten to mention."

Oh, here it comes, I thought, clenching my jaw until it ached. *There's always a catch when it comes to my sister.*

Angelika cleared her throat and had the grace to hurriedly look away when she met my suspicious glare.

"Nothing horrible," she said determinedly, "it's just that they got an invitation to add a few dates to the beginning of their tour. They haven't said yes yet, of course, but if you could take Adeline sooner then they'd be able to make that happen."

"How much sooner?"

"Umm, like at the end of this week?" She clasped her hands together and looked at Lorne with a convincing smile. "Think of it this way, she'll be here to help when the horses arrive. Winter is the hardest time, right? Wouldn't it be better if she came now rather than in spring? And she's used to cold winters. I bet she'll be a lot of help."

"Of course, that's fine," Julie said quickly before I could protest. "The rooms are all ready, aren't they, Bree?"

"Yes," I said with a sigh. "they're all ready. But the hall still needs it's final coats of paint."

I had spent the last few months slowly remodeling the upstairs bedrooms and hallway. It had gone quickly when Nicholas had been home to keep me company and help with the work.

But as soon as he went back to his dorm at the university my progress had slowed considerably. It just wasn't the same without him. Nicholas had a way of making everything fun and he kept me laughing. Without him, I just didn't seem to have the motivation to finish.

My dad had been around to help with the first part of the renovations, too. But lately, he'd been trying to get some of his model sets finished and shipped halfway around the world for a big travelling museum exhibit. So, he didn't have much time to hang out around here lately, either.

"That would be amazing," Angelika said, her eyes lighting up, "but only if it's not too much trouble, of course."

Of course not, I thought with a sigh. But when I looked around at Lorne and Julie's kind, earnest expressions, I felt guilty all over again. Why was I feeling so petty about this girl coming? After all, Lorne and Julie had helped me when I'd had zero experience with horses. That should make me feel *more* generous to help other people, not less.

CHAPTER 4

BREE

*A*ngelika left soon after, giving me a big grateful hug on her way out the door and thanking me about a dozen times even though I hadn't been all that helpful.

As soon as she was gone, I ran upstairs to have that scalding hot shower I'd been longing for. I stayed under the hot water as long as I could and then I padded to my room, cranked the baseboard heater to the hottest setting, and crawled into bed, pulling the thick covers up to my shoulders and snuggling inside. After a moment I pulled my laptop over beside me and fired it up.

I still had an entire blog to finish by the end of the week but right then, I wanted to do a little snooping about our new houseguest.

The Wilsons, I typed in and was rewarded instantly with a page full of hits.

I clicked on the first link, which turned out to be an unbelievably detailed, six-page Wikipedia entry that charted their entire career starting from when the kids were small. The oldest sister,

Hope Wilson, someone I'd never heard of had an entire page written about her.

It must have been quite the fan who wrote this, I thought, *or someone with a lot of spare time on their hands.* The group was hardly that famous or that interesting. Only one or two of their songs had even made it to the radio so I was surprised that their biography was that detailed.

There were a handful of photos and most of them featured the older sister posing with her parents, their manager, or the other kids. The earlier photos showed a hippy-looking family all dressed in long skirts, with bare feet and flower crowns on their heads. There were lots of tambourines and everyone wore wide-eyed earnest expressions.

Were they in some sort of religious cult? I wondered, frowning at a photo of a wild-looking toddler holding a set of brass cowbells.

But the modern-day photos had a more polished look. They were wearing shoes, the clothes they wore had been updated and their hair, though still long and blonde, was neatly trimmed and styled. There was not a flower crown to be seen.

Now, which one is ours? I thought, scrolling slowly through the page again. Her name was listed and there was a brief biography that mentioned her role in saving the kids from the fire, but there wasn't a photo of her.

Finally, I found a group photo that had all their names on it, and I searched the rows for Adeline. At first glance, she didn't really stand out from the others. Her smile was bland, her eyes bright. She stood with two young kids in front of her, her hands held protectively on their shoulders. She looked about thirteen years old in the photo so it must have been a few years before their fire.

"All right, let's see what you guys sound like."

I backed out of the Wikipedia entry and a quick search brought up a handful of videos. I pulled up one of the older videos, one from their Canadian Talent audition, and turned the sound up. Yep, just like I'd thought, kind of sweet and harmonious religious type music. It wasn't my thing, but the sound was pleasant enough, although a little boring. There were lots of fiddles and guitars. All their voices blended seamlessly.

I stopped the video halfway through and kept scrolling. Partway down the page there were suddenly a few news headlines about the fire.

Girl saves siblings from blazing inferno.

Heroic teen leads children to safety.

I clicked open the first article. There was a colour photo right at the top of a smiling Adeline in her hospital bed surrounded by a sea of also-smiling faces. Her eyes were calm and sparkling and she didn't look like someone who'd had a near-death experience.

Local singing sensation, Adeline and her musical family might have lost their home, but they still have a lot to be grateful for.

Last week, their family home was engulfed in flames due to faulty wiring, leaving the family of ten to escape with only the clothes on their backs.

Thanks to middle child Adeline, all the children were able to get out of the home safely.

"It all happened so fast. We were incredibly lucky that nobody was hurt or worse," their mother Charity told news reporters today. "Adeline is the reason why our younger babies made it out alive. She is our hero, our miracle."

Adeline is no stranger to the spotlight. She comes from a family of singing talents who have performed throughout the province since the

*kids were toddlers. A few years ago, they were semi-finalists in Cana-
dian Talent. Recently, Adeline's voice was the winner of a province-wide
contest and she was able to spend a week at an exclusive music camp
honing her skills. We expect great things of this young star.*

*Although she can't talk yet due to smoke inhalation and damage to
her throat, Adeline is expected to make a full recovery and be back in
top form in no time.*

*We look forward to seeing what the future holds for this brave young
woman.*

"Wow," I said, sitting up on my bed and stretching out my
shoulder muscles.

I scrolled back up to look at the photo. I couldn't help
admiring how close-knit the family seemed to be. I mean, my
parents loved me, but I'd never seen them look at me like that.
Like I was a shining star. Although, I guess I'd never saved
anyone from a burning building, either.

The kids and parents all looked pretty much alike. Blonde
hair, blue eyes, radiant, wholesome expressions.

Well, all except that one, I thought, catching sight of an older
girl right at the top of the photo. She was half-out of the frame
almost as if she'd tried to turn away from the photographer at the
last minute. She wasn't looking at the camera, she was gazing
down toward her heroic sister. And her dark, almost angry
expression wasn't radiant at all.

I shivered a little and pulled the blanket closer around my
shoulders.

I did one last search and finally found a more recent video,
one that would have been taken after the fire.

It was a bad cell phone video that had been taken from the
middle of the audience in a larger stadium. The stage was just a
small square in the middle of the screen. There were even
people's heads partially blocking the view.

The sound was much different than their earlier music and
this time I heard Adeline's voice weaving around the others.

"Wow," I said out loud. I knew now exactly what Angelika had meant. There was something different and special about it, but it didn't exactly blend in smoothly with the rest of the family.

Her voice had a haunting quality to it that kept me glued to the screen. Suddenly there was some sort of glitch in the video and a yowl of microphone feedback from the stage. The sound cut out and when it came back again, Adeline's voice was gone, although the rest of them were still singing

Interesting, I thought, setting my laptop aside.

I couldn't imagine what it would be like having a career that included my parents and Angelika. The four of us could hardly spend an hour in the same room together let alone work and live together full time. Even thinking about it was exhausting.

Suddenly, I didn't begrudge this girl's arrival quite so much.

CHAPTER 5

ADIE

*T*he night of the fire changed everything for me. And though it later led to good things, like going to October Horses and meeting Bree and Ace, at the time it was incredibly painful.

There is a lot of inspiring talk that goes around about people rising up from the ashes of their ruined careers, or their damaged bodies, or their destroyed relationships like transformed golden Phoenixes. Everyone loves an underdog survivor after all.

But what they neglect to mention is how darn messy and awful that transformation is. How having a great loss strips away all the things you know about yourself, about your faith, and even your connections to the people you love.

My voice was not the worst thing I lost in the aftermath of that fire.

There were five of us sharing the drafty attic space in our old three-story farmhouse. My parents and my three older siblings, Hope, Micah and Mariam, had rooms on the floor below ours while the rest of us shared three bedrooms, a sprawling playroom and a tiny bathroom between us.

The attic was cold in the winter and sweltering in the summer, but we loved it up there. It was like our own little world. There were skylights in each room that let the light shine in. And, on clear nights, you could lie on your bed and watch the bright stars shining overhead in a velvety black sky.

It was like our own little oasis. The two sets of stairs that needed to be climbed to reach our attic was enough to keep our parents and older siblings nicely out of our business for the most part.

As the oldest child in the attic, I should have had my own room and not had to share. But my brother was the only boy on that floor and my younger sister, Florentine, was terrified to sleep by herself. So, Grady got the single bedroom in the middle, I shared with Flora, and the twins, Izzy and Ivy, had the small bedroom on the end, the one with the window that overlooked the screened porch below us.

The farmhouse was old and rambling with a dark and slightly terrifying cold-cellar at the bottom. Above that was the sprawling main floor with a living room, kitchen, and the music studio, where we spent most of our time. Then the bedrooms on the second floor where the rest of my family lived and, at the top of the house, there was us.

Everyone said later that if I hadn't woken up at exactly the right moment that we probably wouldn't have survived. The house was made of dry, ancient wood, and once the fire started, it was only a matter of minutes before the top of the house was engulfed.

They said that the fire began in the walls of the stairwell that led to the floor below us. The ancient wiring had finally given out and sparked the walls and old insulation.

I was normally a heavy sleeper, because in a house with eight kids you had to be, so there really wasn't any rational reason that I woke up at all.

I was in the middle of the nicest dream. I was lying in a patch of sunlight out in the orchard just peacefully reading a book without anyone bothering me. And I guess when you have four younger siblings who are always demanding attention, and a full-time singing career with your family, then dreams of quiet solitude are about as perfect as it gets.

I don't even remember what book I was dreaming about but I do know that I was really into it. It was like the best book ever written. And then all of a sudden, I looked up, and there was this horse standing there right beside me.

He was tall and dark, and looked nothing like our old, shaggy pony Teddy, who we'd lost the year before. But he had the same sort of wise, kind *feel* to him that Teddy had.

We just stared at each other for ages, not even moving. And, despite the fact that nothing at all was happening, I felt this incredible sense of peace and calm wash over me.

You need to wake up.

The voice sounded in my head, low and musical, like a cello. It was beautiful, and the sound vibrated through me like my whole body was suddenly made of music.

I could have happily stayed in that dream forever. But the next second there was a whooshing feeling as if I were moving at a great speed. Suddenly, I was in my bed fully awake. Not groggy with sleep like I normally would be, but fully alert and sitting up, my heart pounding.

The feeling of peace dissipated as my senses went into high alert. I thought I heard voices yelling from a distance. And there was a strange snapping and whooshing sound coming from the hall. And though there wasn't any smoke in our room yet, the air just tasted bad. Acrid and full of chemicals. Something was terribly wrong.

Don't panic, the dream voice said in my head. *Stay calm.*

Another surge of that feeling of peace washed over me again, and I felt the tingle of the music running through my body, quiet but powerful.

There is a fire, but you can handle this. Stay low, keep moving. Try not to breathe the smoke. Get your sister.

I didn't think to question the fact that I was hearing voices. I knew I needed to move fast.

Smoke was wafting in over the top of our bedroom door now. I pulled the neck of my t-shirt up so it covered my mouth and nose and crawled toward my little sister's bed.

The floorboards were rough under my hands and knees as I reached Flora's bed and shook her awake. She, like most of us, slept like a log too, and it took me precious seconds to make sure she was really up.

"What's happening?" she said sleepily, rubbing her eyes and looking around in bewilderment.

"We're going to be fine," I told her firmly, "but you need to stay right with me, okay? We need to keep moving."

She nodded at me, not saying another word, her eyes wide. She clutched her stuffed bear in one hand and the leg of my pajamas in the other and scrambled after me as we crawled across the floor.

From down below us came a crashing, splintering noise, and then the sound of screaming.

Mom, I thought, my heart constricting and my eyes burning with tears. I brushed them away quickly and kept going.

Black, bitter smoke billowed down the hall over our heads, and the crackling sound was much louder out here than it had been in our room.

Grady's room was next to ours and when I pushed open his door, I found him sitting on his bed fully awake staring at us with a frightened, hollow expression. There were dark circles under his eyes and his hair stood up in all directions.

"What's going on?" he said, his voice coming out hard and tense.

"There's a fire," I said, as calmly as I could, "so we need to get out of here now."

He nodded wordlessly and grabbed his guitar, slinging it over his shoulder.

Why didn't I think of bringing anything? I thought, picturing my own beautiful guitar propped up on its stand beside my bed.

There isn't time for that, the voice in my head said firmly, *you need to get the twins.*

By the time we were back out in the hall and headed for my sister's room, the far end of the house was cracking, popping, and groaning like it was coming apart at the seams.

My sisters were already awake, just like Grady had been, sitting together on one bed with their arms wrapped around each other for comfort.

"Adie, we knew you'd come to get us," Ivy said, her voice coming out in a terrified gasp.

The little girl's room was as far away from the fire as we could possibly get but it still didn't feel far enough. My heart hammered with terror as I looked around wildly and tried to figure out what to do.

Nobody cried. Not even a whimper. They all looked at me with impossibly wide eyes full of terror. But that fear was also mixed with the certainty that no matter how bad this looked, I would find a way to make everything okay.

They trusted me completely. Somehow, I had to get them all out.

The linen closet is just out in the hall, the voice said calmly. *Gather all the sheets you can. You're going to tie them together and go out the window. You can drop down to the porch roof from there, and then you're going to climb down that big oak tree and reach the ground safely. Do this now.*

"Stay here," I told the kids. "I'll be right back. Grady, see if you can open the window. And keep the door shut."

Every inch of me protested at going back out into the smoky, toxic hallway. I didn't want to be the one in charge who had to do the hard things. I wanted to wait for someone else to come and rescue us. But there was only me.

A wall of heat and smoke hit me when I opened the door. The air was so thick that it was like pushing through something half-solid. It felt hot and dangerous against my skin. My eyes and throat burned.

Flattening myself to the ground, I crawled out into the hall-way, slamming the bedroom door behind me.

The closet was just across from me, hardly three steps, but it felt like miles to get there. Wood crackled and popped, and outside I could hear the yard dogs frantically barking their alarm. Breaking glass sounded from somewhere in the house.

The wooden closet door had a habit of swelling shut and sticking, and I had to use all my might to wrench it free. The smoke billowed thickly above me but even though I couldn't see them, I knew the sheets were on the top shelf. I didn't have a choice but to clamp my eyes shut, hold my breath, and stand up to claw out as many sheets as I could.

I just knocked anything within reach onto the floor and then dropped down as fast as I could. My eyes were stinging so badly that I could hardly open them, and my throat and lungs burned. I coughed and wheezed my way back to the bedroom with my armload of sheets, hoping that I'd grabbed enough of them to make a long-enough rope.

"I had to smash it," Grady said, his eyes wide and his face an ashy white colour. He held the twin's heavy lamp in both hands. "It wouldn't open."

Shards of glass littered the floor in all directions and bits of it still clung to the edges of the window frame. Luckily all the little girls and their bare feet were sitting on the nearest bed.

"Good job," I said, "finish breaking the small pieces out of the window. Izzy, grab the blankets off your beds and throw them to me. Don't step on the floor. I'm going to tie these sheets together."

I tied as quickly as I could. Hoping my knots would hold. Hoping my makeshift rope would be long enough, and hoping I'd have enough strength to support everyone as they climbed down it.

The second Grady was done smashing at the window, I grabbed the thick duvets that the twins had tossed onto the floor beside their beds. I draped them hurriedly across the floor and the windowsill so that hopefully nobody would get cut as we escaped.

I winced and tried not to yelp as I felt tiny slivers of glass pricking into my feet.

The sheets fell out the window in heavy loops and there was a reassuring thud as the first knot hit the roof below. I would have more than enough.

Hurry, the dream voice in my head said, *you're almost out of time.*

"Okay, come on, Flora," I called, "you're first, you can do this."

But instead of obeying she burst into tears and grabbed onto the twins, sobbing hysterically.

"Noooooo," she wailed, "Grady goes first."

"Look, this won't work," Grady said firmly, "You can't hold the rope, Adie. You won't be able to climb down yourself. We need to tie the rope to the bed."

"But then it might not be long enough."

"It will be. Or we'll have to jump a little bit. Come on, let's push the bed to the window."

We don't have time for this, I thought desperately, watching the black smoke billow in over our heads. *It's going to be too late.*

Somewhere in the night, sirens wailed, and I could hear far away shouts and the dogs still barking.

The twins' window overlooked the thickest, wooded part of the property, but as I looked outside into the darkness, I could see the entire sky over our heads and the tops of the trees lit up with an eerie orange glow.

We pushed the ancient wooden bed over to the window and I tied and double-tied the knot to the slatted headboard, my fingers shaking hard the whole time.

"Go first, Grady," I said, peering out the window at the makeshift rope, "then I'll send the kids down to you. I might need to carry Flora."

"Right," he said, then hesitated for a second. "Adie, I have to tell you something—"

"Grady, you have to go. Tell me later. I'll meet you down below. I promise."

He shut his mouth abruptly and then climbed out onto the windowsill, clutching the rope between both hands until his knuckles went white.

"Come over here, girls," I ordered, "be careful of the glass. I want you to watch how Grady does this. See how he climbs down. It's easy. You just have to be brave."

They reluctantly came over to stand beside me, fingers clutching nervously at my clothes. Flora quietly stifling her sobs.

I kept both hands on the rope just in case and prayed hard the whole time as Grady lowered himself over the edge and disappeared into the darkness. I held my breath until he made it to the porch roof, landing with a thud.

"It worked," he called, "come on Ivy, you're next."

She didn't even argue, just took a deep breath, and let me help her up onto the windowsill. I held her tightly until she had both hands on the rope and then I watched anxiously as she silently made her way down.

When she reached the bottom, she sat down hard on the roof and then waved up at us wildly with both hands to show us she was all right.

"Right, Izzy, you can do this."

I kept hold of her in the same way I had her sister and, although she moved much more slowly and I could hear her crying quietly to herself, she finally made it to the bottom, too.

"Right, your turn, Flora. Can you climb down yourself or do you want me to carry you?" I asked, although I really had no idea how I'd manage to get both of us down.

"I can do it myself," she said. "I'm a better climber than the twins are. Remember the time I climbed that—"

"Yes, you're an excellent climber," I interrupted as the door behind us suddenly made a violent popping noise. "Now, fast as you can. Here's the rope, hold on tight. Grady is right below you and I'll be right behind you. The second you reach the roof I want you all to run for the tree, okay. You tell Grady that. Don't wait for me. I'll be right behind you."

"Okay." She nodded firmly. She'd stopped crying and she didn't even look scared anymore. She gritted her jaw with determination and launched herself at the window. I barely had time to guide her on the rope. She wasn't lying. She climbed down that rope like a monkey, and she had barely hit the porch roof before she was yelling at her sisters and heading directly for the tree.

Good girl, Flora, I whispered thankfully under my breath. And then it was my turn. Just as I threw my leg outside the windowsill the entire ceiling over my head erupted into flame. For a second, I was mesmerized as it moved toward me in a shimmering wave and then I was moving.

Hand over fist I shimmied down the makeshift rope, feeling my way down until I hit the roof. I looked around for the kids in a panic, but thankfully they had listened to me and had already climbed for safety.

There was a whooshing noise and the entire third floor went up like a candle. I turned and ran as fast as I could for the tree. There was a loud groaning noise over my head, and I heard something heavy crash to the roof beside me.

I screamed and dove for the tree, but I was just a second too late. Something hard hit me from behind and I was knocked sideways. Flames licked close to my skin. The smell of burning filled my lungs and I gasped, sucking desperately for air. It was like breathing in a scorching desert of heat. My lungs bucked and spasmed in protest.

Fight, the voice in my head said, *fight as hard as you can.*

With a supreme effort, I heaved whatever piece of half-burned debris that had fallen on me to the side and crawled toward that welcoming tree.

I half-fell, half-climbed down the trunk, barely feeling the branches tearing at my hair, my clothes and my bare skin as I clambered past them.

I nearly sobbed when my feet hit the soft grass at the base of the tree. I sat down hard, and I probably would have stayed there forever if there hadn't been another crashing noise overhead.

I got up and ran as fast as I could on my throbbing feet, running through the woods until they merged with the driveway a few hundred feet from the house. I skidded to a stop, narrowly missing a collision with a parked firetruck.

Dozens of them lined the driveway. Lights flashed and there was a confusion of yelling and water flying at our burning house from all angles. I stared, transfixed in horror. It was my home, a place I'd spent most of my childhood, the place of so many good memories. And it was all being destroyed right in front of my eyes.

Where is everyone? I thought, looking around wildly. Surely, they'd all made it out safely. They had to be all right.

"Adeline!" It was my mother's scream, and I began running toward the sound as fast as my battered feet would carry me.

And suddenly, there they were, all around me, hugging, laughing, crying. The kids crowded against me. My throat hurt too much for me to say anything at all. I could only stand there and sob in relief.

"We're all safe," my dad said as he crushed me in a tight hug. "And we are so, so proud of you. You're a hero, Adie."

It was a strange experience being surrounded by the love of my amazing family while our house burned down in front of us. It was like the worst thing and the best thing happening at the same time.

All that matters is that we're together, I thought, tears streaming down my face. *Nothing else matters at all.*

But as I looked around, I saw that Hope hadn't been a part of our group hug. She was standing a few feet away, staring at our house with her eyes glittering in the reflection of the flames. And I thought, just for a second, there was a ghost of a smile on her face.

CHAPTER 6

BREE

*T*hat night, after the final horse chores were done and the supper dishes had been washed and put away, I skipped the usual after-dinner TV watching with Lorne and Julie and wearily headed upstairs.

I was bone-tired but I was hoping to get at least the first coat of paint on the hallway before our new working student arrived.

"Are you sure you're doing okay?" Julie called after me worriedly. "Don't you want dessert?"

"No thanks," I said quickly. Dessert that night had been ice cream and there was no way I was putting anything frozen in my body until at least August. "I just want to get the hall finished before the new girl comes."

"I could help if you like," Julie said studying my face with a frown. "I don't want you getting overworked."

"I've got it. Don't worry, Julie."

The long hallway was dingy without paint and was not well-lit at the best of times. So, my first step was to open the doors to all the rooms and turn every single light on so at least I had enough light to see by.

The upper floor in Julie's house was always about three degrees colder than the lower one. Despite the law that hot air was supposed to rise, the heat hardly seemed to reach the stairwell before leaking away through the single pane windows into the wintery night.

There were tiny baseboard heaters in each bedroom, and if you shut yourself in your room before going to bed and cranked the heat to the maximum then you might avoid freezing to death overnight.

Luckily, way back at the beginning of this project, my dad had brought me a slightly scary plug-in metal heater that glowed orange and had an internal fan that blasted warmth in an unending stream. If you had it pointed right at you, it was like standing in a sauna.

"Maybe just don't leave that unattended," he'd told me, looking at it a little nervously. "I found it in our basement, and I can't remember how old it is."

Despite that sketchy endorsement, I'd taken to setting the little heater a few feet away from where I was working and cranking it as high as it could go. It probably helped the paint dry faster, too.

Perfect, I thought, feeling my muscles relax as soon as the delicious blast of heat hit me.

It wasn't hard to fall into a rhythm once I'd started. The *sploosh* of the roller hitting the tray, and then the sticky sound the paint made as I worked my way steadily across the walls from top to bottom was soothing.

When I'd first begun working on the renovations, my arms would ache all the time from having to hold the roller upwards for so long. But over time, I'd grown much stronger and the job had become almost effortless. And I'd grown much more skilled at it, too. There were no more random blobs of paint to clean up afterwards or accidental streaks on the ceiling.

Maybe being a house painter will be my back-up career if the horse and the writing thing falls through, I thought, stopping to admire the section of hall I'd just finished. *At least, if I live long enough to have a career, that is.*

The only problem with doing this by myself was that when I was alone, my thoughts kept drifting to the things I didn't like thinking about. The thoughts I could mostly avoid when I was working with the horses or surrounded by other people. As long as I kept busy, there wasn't any time to dwell on worries. But as soon as I was alone, they all came flooding back.

Am I going to die? Will Ace really be sound? Why doesn't Nicholas like me?

This last thought was a tricky one.

My logical, practical side had already come to terms with the fact that Nicholas and I were only destined to be friends. So why was it so much harder to make my heart fall into line? The sooner I stopped thinking about him, the happier I would be.

He was one of those nice, happy guys that everyone loved and wanted to be around. He was probably at some university party surrounded by nice, smart girls right now. While I was here all alone—

"Breanna?"

I jerked and nearly dropped the freshly loaded paint roller onto the floor.

"Dad, you scared me," I gasped, setting the roller down carefully in its tray. "What on earth are you doing here so late?"

"Is it late?" He looked at his watch. "It's eight o 'clock, kiddo, not midnight. I just wanted to check up and see how you're doing."

"Julie called you, didn't she?" I said, raising an eyebrow at him. He looked like he'd just come from his workshop. His hair stood up in all directions and he was still in his grubby paint-stained jeans.

"Ah, well, you caught me. She did. She's a bit worried about you."

"I know," I said with a sigh. There was no use pretending with my dad. He'd been through the whole near-death experience with me, so he pretty much saw through me no matter what.

"You look all right, maybe a little pale."

"Yeah, I think I'm okay physically. I mean I'm tired and sore, but I think that's just from all the farm work. I'm just, I don't know …"

I didn't really know how to explain it to him.

"A little winter blues maybe," he said kindly, "your mother gets that way too right about now."

"She does? I never noticed."

"Well, she's good at keeping herself busy so that nobody notices. But you can always tell that she is kind of holding her breath until spring hits. The second that it does, she sort of inhales and comes alive again. You can time it like clockwork."

I thought back to my mom being constantly in the kitchen, always cooking up new recipes and stocking the freezer with more food than a family could possibly eat. Or obsessively cleaning the house.

When we were young, she'd practically been Angelika's private chauffer driving her off to one class after another. Had that all been just to keep herself busy? To keep herself from thinking?

"Okay," I said slowly. "So, do you have any suggestions then?"

"Well, first step is to make an appointment with Dr. Grace, I think. Not that I think there's anything wrong," he added hurriedly, "but feeling blue might mean that the medications need to be altered. She's the expert, after all."

"Yeah, I suppose."

"I can come with you if you like. Or perhaps Nicholas could drive you."

Nicholas was enrolled at the same university where my dad taught, and my dad pretty much thought he walked on water. I knew that he was hoping that we'd conveniently end up together.

"I don't think that's going to happen, Dad," I said, looking away quickly. "He's pretty busy with school. He doesn't need to worry about me."

"Ah," he said, "I see."

There was a short, awkward silence, and I picked up the roller again to have something to do with my hands.

"Well, this hallway isn't going to paint itself, I suppose. Where are your extra rollers?"

"Dad, you don't have to help me. I know you have your own projects due."

"Well, I need a break from that. Nothing would make me happier than to help you finally finish this hallway. Hopefully when we're done Julie doesn't suggest we start renovating the downstairs floor of the house, too."

My mood lightened a lot when there were two of us working and any lingering awkwardness faded after a few minutes. Soon, we were chatting away companionably about all sorts of things. And singing along to the occasional good song on the radio my dad had dragged out from my room.

When we were done and the whole hall was coated in its first glossy layer of paint, I felt better than I had in ages. As if a weight had been lifted from my shoulders.

"Thanks so much for coming to keep me company, Dad," I said, wrapping him in a quick hug just as he was leaving. "I can't believe the first coat is finally done. It looks amazing."

"Any time. And let me know when you've made your appointment with Dr. Grace. I wouldn't mind tagging along if you'd like the company."

"Okay, I will. I'll call her this week. Say hi to mom for me."

CHAPTER 7

BREE

"*W*hat do you mean the girl doesn't sing anymore?" Chloe asked a few days later when we were in the barn brushing horses. I had been hurriedly filling her in about our new upcoming house guest since I'd roped Chloe into going to pick her up with me.

The world outside was too icy to turn anyone out once again, so Chloe and I had decided to spend our morning grooming all the horses, including all the seniors. We had some time to kill until we had to go pick up Adeline from the bus depot.

"I don't know, that's what Angelika said. She seemed fine in the videos that I watched. And that was after the fire."

"Hmm, maybe she had a relapse of some sort."

My breath caught for a second.

Relapse, I thought, hating the word with every fiber of my being. I had made my call to Dr. Grace first thing that morning. Unfortunately, her first appointment spot wasn't for weeks, but she'd booked me in for bloodwork at the lab in the meantime.

I was fairly sure that I was overreacting and was going to be completely fine. But there was a small, dark part of me that was filled with terror at the unknown. What if—?

I narrowed my focus to concentrate on picking out Ace's long, dark tail strand by strand. It was much too cold to bathe him, but I'd covered his tail in a thick dousing of detangler and now most of the strands fell like a curtain against his shiny flanks. I just had a handful of tangles to work out.

He snorted happily, glad for the attention even though he was stuck inside yet again.

"I wish it was me coming to live here instead of her, though," Chloe said. "My mom is being ridiculous about this summer. She basically said that if I move out then she won't pay for my school next year. And I wouldn't get paid much here for being a working student so it wouldn't be like I could save up."

"Except for getting room and board and to ride the horses and have free lessons," I reminded her.

"I know, I know. I'm not complaining. But that wouldn't help me pay for university, right? I'd have to take out a student loan or something. Or skip a year of school maybe and take off a year to ride."

She absently patted Cooper's freshly brushed chestnut neck and threw his blanket back on. "I love riding more than anything. But my parents are really pushing me to go to a local college so I can live at home and still help my mom out. I have no idea what to do."

"If you aren't positive about what you want to study in school then I would pick riding, for sure," I said seriously. "I wish I'd made a different choice when it came time to go to university. I just went because that seemed like the next logical step, but I didn't really know what I wanted at the time. I should have taken a year to travel, or work, and to find out what I was meant to do in life. I could have saved myself a lot of grief and my parents a lot of money."

"Hmm," Chloe said, "I'm not sure if my parents would go for that. My mom has it all planned out that I'll be around on the weekends and at night to babysit my little brothers next winter. She's working overtime on her cake-making business since the divorce, and I think it's making her a little crazy. She pretty much wants me to live with her forever. Each time I bring up leaving, she accuses me of abandoning her just like my dad did."

Her voice caught and she broke off abruptly.

I tossed my brush into the grooming tote and turned around to study her. "Yikes, I'm so sorry, Chloe. I had no idea things were that bad."

"Yeah, it's no big deal," she said, not meeting my eyes. "Don't worry, I'll figure it out somehow."

"I know, but—"

"What time is she coming again?" Chloe interrupted.

"Her bus should be arriving in a couple of hours. You're still coming with me, right? I feel like I'm going to need some back up. I've never babysat in my life."

"Oh, come on, she's sixteen, she's really not that much younger than us. And I'm sure you were stuck looking after your younger sister all the time."

"Actually, I wasn't," I said thoughtfully. "We didn't really get along and she was always off doing important things like becoming famous. I don't think our parents trusted us to be alone together anyway. We were pretty awful to each other when we were teenagers."

"Aw, that's too bad. I mean, my brothers are a pain, but we still have fun together. I just don't want to be forced to look after them as a full-time, unpaid nanny."

"Angelika and I are a work in progress," I said, laughing. "We have a lot of time to make up for, I guess. Hopefully, I don't regret taking this new girl on for her."

. . .

A few hours later we were sitting outside a dingy bus terminal. There was no sign of our new guest and I wondered if Angelika had gotten it all wrong. Maybe the girl had changed her mind and wasn't coming at all. Or maybe she'd mixed up the dates.

"Do you think we'll even recognize her?" I asked, tapping my fingers nervously on the wheel of Lorne's car. It was twenty minutes past the hour. The bus terminal wasn't in the best part of town, and I'd gotten it into my head that the sketchy-looking man loitering nearby was just waiting for his chance to rob us.

"She can't have changed that much in the few months since her concert video," Chloe said. "Although it's hard to tell what anyone looks like when they're bundled in winter gear up to their eyeballs."

Chloe took a sip of her coffee and glanced down at the car clock again.

A few busses had already pulled up and parked, their air brakes squealing and hissing loudly, exhaust steaming white clouds into the cold air. So far nobody looking like our new guest had appeared.

"Do you think she's waiting inside the building?" I asked worriedly. I would hate to have to go back and explain to Lorne and Julie that we'd lost our first working student before she'd even arrived. "I have to be home in an hour to interview Slate's mom for my blog. I wonder if I should go look for her."

"There, that's her. I think." Chloe pointed a mittened hand in the direction of the last bus. A pale, thin girl stood off to one side. She looked young and a little lost.

"Yeah, I think so, too. Let's go."

We hopped out and I waved to the girl as we crossed the parking lot. I pasted a smile on my face, doing my best to look like a good farm ambassador.

As soon as she recognized us, it was like someone had flicked a switch. Her posture changed and a wide smile lit up her face.

Her lost expression dissolved, and she turned confidently toward us.

"Hello," she said, stepping forward boldly and holding her hand out for us to shake. "I'm Adeline Wilson and I appreciate this fantastic opportunity you're giving me. I'm excited to be here."

Her voice was low and gravelly, which seemed out of place in such a tiny person. She paused for breath, and Chloe and I exchanged a quick glance.

"Er, hello ..." I began.

"You must be Bree," she went on, "Angelika told me all about you and I have read every issue of your blog. Thank you so much for having me stay."

"Ah, you're welcome?" I said, a little taken aback. "I mean yes, it's nice to meet you, too. This is Chloe."

"Oh, you ride Dragon. I loved reading Bree's stories about you. I can't wait to meet all the horses."

"Always glad to meet a fan of Dragon's," Chloe said, grinning.

"Well, let's go warm up in the car," I said, relieved at how easy this was going. Adeline seemed a lot older than I'd expected. I didn't have any experience with teenagers, but she seemed to be pretty self-sufficient. She acted a lot more mature than I had at that age, that was for sure. "I got you a hot chocolate because I wasn't sure if you liked coffee or not."

"Thanks, I like anything, really. But hot chocolate sounds nice. I appreciate you thinking of me."

We walked back to the car while I vowed to up my farm ambassador game. Adie was pretty much the politest person I'd ever met. My parents would have loved to have had a kid like that. Between Angelika's constant dramatic outbursts and me spending hours sulking in my room, we hadn't given much thought to polishing our social skills when we were this girl's age.

She asked polite questions about the farm on the way back

and told us again how appreciative she was that we were taking her in.

"I promise to earn my keep," she said firmly. "I am used to hard work and pitching in."

"You must be looking forward to not having to babysit all your younger brothers and sisters," Chloe joked. "I can't imagine what it must be like having *eight* kids in my family."

Adie drew a sudden breath in the back seat, and I glanced in the rear-view mirror, wondering if she'd burned herself on her hot chocolate or something.

She was staring intently out the window, biting her lip. Her professional exterior had cracked a little and she suddenly looked like she was trying not to cry.

"Adie?" I said. "Are you okay?"

"Um …" she took a deep breath and the pain on her face smoothed away like magic. She smiled at me reassuringly. "Yes, of course I am. Thank you for asking. I've just … I've never been away from my family for long before. It's sort of been my job to take care of the little kids, and this will be my first time away from them. Except for when I was in the hospital."

She broke off and sat up straight in her seat, a determined look crossing her face. "But this was the best decision for everyone and I'm lucky to be here. This is a great opportunity. Thanks again."

Chloe and I exchanged another glance.

"Um, yes, of course. We're happy to have you here. So, how do you know my sister?"

"Oh, well, I don't exactly *know* her," Adie said. "I really just met her the one time. She was amazing, though. You're really lucky to have her as a sister."

"You only met her once?" I asked incredulously, my voice rising a few pitches.

She met my startled glance in the rear-view mirror and then looked hastily away.

"I mean, we move in some of the same circles, I guess, and I've talked to her on the phone. Once. My parents have talked to her more, though."

She broke off and I sat there simmering in silence, wondering how on earth Angelika had managed to con me into taking on a stranger that she'd only met *once,* for heaven's sake. She'd made it sound like this kid was her best friend. And why on earth had she wanted this girl to come here in the first place? It didn't make sense.

I looked in the mirror again and took in Adie's flushed expression and trembling lower lip.

It's not her fault, I reminded myself firmly, *this is on Angelika, not her. She's a guest and I shouldn't take it out on her.*

"You'll love the farm," I said quickly to break the silence. "Julie and Lorne are really nice. They've honestly become like second parents to me. Lorne tries to act all gruff and grumpy, but he's really sweet, and Julie knows everything about horses and she's so kind. And the horses are amazing. Ace is my favourite of course, but Nipper and Bear are close seconds."

"I loved your article on Bear," Adie said softly. "He looked so nice in the pictures."

"You can ride him once the snow melts. I know Julie will give you lessons. There is one thing about Julie that I should mention, though. I don't talk about it in the blog at all, but she has some scars and burns on her face and body."

"Burns?" Adie looked up quickly. "Was she in a house fire like me?"

"She was in a car accident a long time ago, but it took her a lot of time and surgeries to recover. It still hurts sometimes, and she doesn't ride anymore. Although she does everything else.

"She's a bit shy around new people. You won't even notice the scars once you spend a little time with her but just … just don't stare if you can help it."

"No, I won't," Adie said firmly. "I was kept in the burn unit at the hospital for a little bit after our house fire. I didn't even really get burnt, but the smoke and heat had damaged my throat so that's where they put me. I saw a lot of different injuries when I was there, and I know how brave everyone had to be to recover."

"Angelika told me a little bit about you getting hurt," I said slowly, wondering how much I was supposed to know about this girl. I didn't want her to think we'd been gossiping about her. "But not the details or anything. I heard you were a hero though, which sounds amazing. And you were lucky to be able to sing again."

There was another long, strained silence.

"I'm actually giving up singing," Adie said with complete finality. "That part of my life is over."

I wanted to ask so many more questions. The video I'd watched had been taken long after the fire. Adie had definitely been performing in it. Sure, her voice was different, but it had still been singing. So, what had made her stop so abruptly and leave a family it was clearly killing her to be separated from?

Adie perked up again when we reached the farm, breaking the silence with a little squeal of excitement.

"This is it," she said happily, even before we'd slowed down to turn in the driveway. "I recognize it from the pictures."

She pulled out a new-looking phone and took a photo of the sign on the driveway just as I pulled in.

"I promised the kids I'd take tons of pictures for them. They all love animals. I think they all wanted to come."

"Maybe they could visit once their tour thing is over," I said.

Adie sighed. "Yeah, maybe. We'll see what happens. If my dad had his way, they'd extend the tour forever. He loves to be on the road. He was never really thrilled about farm life. That was all my mom and us younger kids."

There was another long silence as we cruised past the barn and headed up the hill.

"We'll go up to the house first to drop your stuff off," I told her, "and then you can see your room and meet Julie. Once you're settled in, you can come down to the barn and meet the horses. The new racehorses haven't arrived yet of course, but you can help us get them settled when they do show up. We have a working student from Scotland coming in a few weeks, too."

"Jeremy." Chloe let out a dreamy sigh beside me, making me laugh. "From Scotland."

"This is just like the pictures online," Adie said excitedly, her sadness banished once again. Her moods changed so fast I could hardly keep up.

She kept her phone out and took pictures of the front of the house, Lorne's car, the porch, and about a dozen of Tom when he came lounging past on his way from the food bowl back to his spot next to the fire.

"I've missed animals so much," she said, kneeling beside him and scratching his chin until his purr was rumbling around the living room like a jet engine. "We had to leave all ours behind when we moved into the city."

"What? Like, you had to sell them?" Chloe said incredulously.

"No, Dad thought the fire was a sign that it was time for us to pursue singing full time. And we couldn't really do that living way out in the country. So, friends of ours moved into the farm after we left for the city. They're builders and they have a big family, too. So, they agreed to do most of the renovations to the upstairs of the house in exchange for living there for free for a few years. The animals just all stayed behind with them. They're really nice people and I know they'll take care of the farm properly, but still ..."

"Yeah, that really sucks," Chloe said. "I'm sorry that happened to you."

Adie's eyes flickered open wide in surprise for a second, and then she shook her head and gave Tom a final pat before standing up again.

"The move was for the good of the family," she said firmly.

"We had to do what was best for everyone."

"Come on," I said, sending Chloe a warning look when she opened her mouth to argue. "Let's go see your room."

Adie followed silently after Chloe and me, as we climbed the stairs.

"I just finished painting the second coat on the hallway," I assured her as she cast a side-long glance at the paint cans and trays piled in one corner. "I just have to finish the trim. It's sort of a winter project. Don't worry, your room is done."

"Oh wow." Adie stood in the open doorway of her room, staring as if frozen.

"Do you like it?" I asked anxiously, not sure how to read her expression.

I'd actually worked hard to make Adie's room look nice. I'd chosen the one across the hall from mine with views of the rolling pastures beyond the house. It was a little bigger than the others and had two windows instead of one.

I'd rooted through the storage room until I'd found a decent set of sheets and one of the new greyish-blue blankets I'd picked out months ago to match the updated paint on the walls.

I'd gone through the stacks of old pictures and paintings that had been stashed in one corner of the storage room until I found a couple of nice ones I'd guessed she might like.

One was an older replica of a painting from the eighteen hundreds of two shiny, bay racehorses standing with their groom in front of an ornate stable.

The other was also older but of a bunch of kids playing in the woods with a pony and a pack of dogs. I figured it might remind her of home since she'd grown up with lots of kids on a farm.

There was a night table beside the bed and a little desk on the far wall. Next to that was a door that led to what was supposed to be a shared bathroom, although right now there wasn't anyone to share it with.

"Like it?" she said breathlessly. "I love it. Is this really all mine?

Like the whole thing?"

"Of course it is. You don't have to share. We all have our own rooms."

"This is wonderful," she said dreamily. "I've never had my own room before."

Chloe and I looked at each other with our eyebrows raised. I guessed that in a house of ten people space was always at a premium. There probably was a lot of sharing.

"I'm so sorry, Adie. I just have to run and do a quick interview at the barn for my blog. You can come hang out if you like or you can get settled in. Or Chloe can show you—"

"Sorry, not me," Chloe said quickly. "I have to get back home to help my mom make her stupid cakes. She took on all these new orders and she can hardly keep up. Really, since the divorce that woman has been losing her mind. I can't wait until I'm out of there."

Adie looked after her with wide eyes as Chloe waved goodbye to us both and trotted down the stairs at top speed.

"Don't mind her," I said reassuringly, "but I really do have to go. My interview won't be too long. Slate's owner Nancy is flying back out to England tomorrow so this is the only time I could schedule it for."

"It's fine. I'll just stay here," Adie said hurriedly. "I'll unpack my stuff and get settled. I should call home and let them know I arrived safely, too."

"Right, well, just yell if you need anything. And feel free to explore the house or come down to the barn whenever you like. You can use the kitchen if you need a snack or a tea or something. Nowhere is off-limits, really. Okay, see you."

I felt bad as I turned and bolted down the stairs in the same direction as Chloe. But Adie seemed pretty self-sufficient and I didn't think it would take her long to settle in. She probably didn't appreciate me hovering over her like she was a little kid anyway.

CHAPTER 8

ADIE

I didn't unpack right away. And I didn't call my family. I just sat down on my bed and stared out the window. The view of the snowy fields was beautiful but I barely saw it. Now that I'd actually arrived, the events of the last few weeks caught up with me and I doubled over, feeling like I'd been punched in the stomach.

I was supposed to be going on tour, I thought, my throat closing up so hard that I could barely breathe. In a week's time, everyone would be leaving our run-down apartment for the last time, getting on our converted bus, and setting off toward the east coast. Setting off for the adventure of a lifetime. Without me.

The thought hurt so much I could hardly stand it. I actually wasn't quite sure how this disastrous turn of events could have happened to me.

The night of that disastrous final concert, the night I'd met Angelika, seemed like it had happened a lifetime ago but really only a few weeks had passed.

The year since the fire had been the longest year of my life. By the time that particular concert came along, I'd been through months of speech therapy and vocal training to get my voice back. I had done exactly what I'd been told to do. I'd practiced precisely as much as I was allowed and then babied my vocal cords the rest of the time.

My post-fire voice was vastly different than what it once had been, but it wasn't awful. I kind of sounded a bit like a young Janis Joplin or Etta James, which was pretty lucky since they were amazing artists.

And fortunately enough, some people really loved the way I sounded. We'd rewritten some of our songs to make my new voice blend in better and we'd had a few fans write glowing reviews online.

Not everyone was on board, though. My sister Hope and our manager Phil had been dead set against me rejoining the group at first. Even my dad had been a little skeptical that I wanted to sing again so soon. But I'd convinced them. Through hard work, endless practice, and a little begging, I'd shown them that I knew exactly where I belonged.

And it had almost worked. Right up until the night of that concert.

Even though I'd performed at a few smaller venues with my family since the accident, this was the biggest concert I'd been part of in over a year. And it was *a very big deal*. As Phil kept reminding me, my job was just to blend in and not draw any attention to myself.

We were one of three opening acts for Angelika and her band. They picked local singers to open for them at every town they played in and we'd been extremely lucky to have been chosen at all.

We'd actually played at a few of the same venues as her before she'd become famous. My parents had spoken to her a little over the years although I'd never done more than nod to her in passing.

I hadn't even known I was going to be included in the concert until a few weeks before the show. Phil and Hope hadn't wanted me there, which was no surprise, but my dad hadn't been too thrilled about it, either.

"I just don't think she's ready," I'd heard him saying to Mom when he thought we were all sleeping. He'd kept his voice low, but the truth was the walls of our run-down city apartment were so thin that you could hear almost everything anyone said and half of what the neighbours said. "She doesn't have perfect control all the time. Some of the fans aren't happy."

"But when she gets it right, she sounds incredible," my mother had said firmly. "She's probably the most talented out of all of us. She'll get there. Our fans will adjust. Bottom line is that we do this as a family or not at all. These children have made a lot of sacrifices to be here. Especially Adie."

He didn't say anything else and the next day my mother brightly announced at breakfast that I would definitely be joining them at the concert.

"I don't think that's a good idea, Charity," Phil had said, wiping his mouth and tossing his dirty napkin down on the table beside his plate. Phil didn't live with us, but he liked to show up uninvited for "breakfast meetings" so he could hoover up vast quantities of my mother's cooking. "She's not ready yet."

"Oh?" My mother had said, raising an eyebrow at him. It was a subtle motion but all of us kids knew that it meant that someone was about to get in trouble. We never crossed her when that eyebrow went up.

Phil must have known that too because he gulped and flashed her an insincere, toothy smile.

"All I'm saying is that you've all worked so hard to develop a sound that audiences really go for. Light and poppy is your brand and you're starting to gain some traction. If you go changing things, then you'll lose your followers. This isn't a good stage in your career to start changing things up."

I looked up to see Phil and my dad exchange a meaningful look.

"Nonsense," my mom had said firmly, "if the songs aren't working the way they are, then we'll just have to write new ones. There is a place for everyone here. And Adie can handle this. You're ready, aren't you, sweetie?"

All eyes at the table turned to look at me and I took a deep breath.

"Yes," I said firmly. "I was born ready for this."

"Well," my mom said, "then that's all the answer we need. This family sticks together. Nobody gets left behind."

She beamed at me, and I tried to smile back, but inwardly my stomach was suddenly churning.

What if I wasn't ready? What if I messed up?

We'd all made so many sacrifices to make our music career work. After the fire, we could have stayed at the farm and slowly fixed up the house. Only the upper floor was completely ruined. The rest of the farmhouse was salvageable.

But instead, we'd had a family meeting and we'd all decided to leave the farm and focus full-time on music. We'd left our home and our pets and our friends behind. We'd moved to a cramped, run-down apartment in Vancouver so that we'd be closer to an actual music scene and have more opportunities to perform. And my dad and my older siblings had all taken minimum wage jobs so they could afford the crazy expensive rent in this city and enough food for all of us.

Am I risking ruining it all for them? I thought anxiously, looking around the room at the people I loved best in the world. Only my older sister Hope and the ever-angry Phil looked resentful, though.

"All or nothing it is, then, Adie," my good-natured older brother, Micah, said. "You've got this."

And I vowed that I would do my absolute best to make sure that everything went off without a hitch.

For the next two weeks, I'd babied my vocal cords like they were newly hatched baby birds. I drank hot lemon and honey by the gallon, I did the world's longest warm-up exercises and vocal exercises to make sure my body was as relaxed as possible before I even dreamed of singing a note.

And finally, the night of the concert had arrived.

Opening for Angelika didn't pay much, but it was excellent exposure and they'd allowed us to set up a little table to sell merchandise alongside the other bands.

Micah and Mariam had designed posters, sent out press releases to everywhere they could think of, and had made us a bunch of promotional t-shirts and things to sell. We would be lucky to break even, but the opportunity to get our name out there was worth it.

Hope, who was in charge of social media, had done a ton of online promotions and had whipped up our limited followers into a frenzy of excitement.

At least a handful of people in this audience would know who we were and would be cheering us on.

"All right, everyone," my mom had said as soon as we were set up in our tiny, shared dressing room, "group prayer." And we all came together with hands held to say a heartfelt thanks for this opportunity.

"There's been a change to the schedule," Phil said, banging the door open and interrupting our peaceful moment.

He swooped in behind us, his cheeks flushed and his forehead sweaty. "We're up first now. There's going to be almost zero time for sound-check before you go on. You're going to have to wing it."

"Seriously?" Hope said, her voice rising up into a shriek. "That's ridiculous. They can't do that to us."

Which was the silliest thing to say because things like that happen all the time when you're a musician.

"They already have. But you've got this." He gave her a lingering glance and quickly squeezed her hand. "Everything is going to be fine."

Hope looked at him with this sickeningly adoring expression, managing to widen her eyes and flutter her lashes at him at the same time. I turned away quickly before I literally threw up right there in front of them. The fact that she and gross Phil had been seeing each other secretly for over a year was something I tried not to dwell on.

But Phil was right. Everything had been fine. Right until the middle of our set. Right until I messed the whole thing up.

It was my favourite song, one I had helped my Dad and Micah write years ago, and there was a part in the middle where the music swelled and our voices rose into this sort of otherworldly chorus that looped and wrapped around each other like intertwined ribbons of sound. I knew exactly where my place in that ribbon was supposed to be.

But suddenly, something strange came over me. That peaceful feeling that I'd felt on the night of the fire came flowing back into my limbs. And it was almost like I felt that comforting presence guiding me again.

Rise up, a voice whispered in my ear. It was that same dream voice, the one that had led me unerringly out of our burning house. I was so startled that I jerked sideways. And when I took my next breath something inside of me shifted and the music just poured out of me, an ocean of sound that I barely even recognized as *me*. A deep, powerful sound from my chest.

Micah turned and flashed me a startled look, but then his surprise changed to encouragement and he grinned and gave me a thumbs up.

And I let it loose.

As my voice swelled up one octave after another, it was the most beautiful, liberating thing I'd ever felt.

Until suddenly, it broke. My throat seized up and the sound ended abruptly in a squeal of feedback from the microphone. It probably sounded as bad as it felt because my entire family faltered and stared at me for just a second before recovering. I swear I even heard the audience gasp, even though that was pretty much impossible to hear over the music.

For a minute, I just stood there on stage in shock, not even sure what had happened.

"Just fake it," Hope hissed at me furiously, so that's what I did. I lip synced my way through the final fifteen minutes of the show, and all the while my throat was burning with pain and the rest of me was shaking with mortification. I couldn't believe I'd done something so reckless. On such an important night, too.

It was a relief to finally be able to stumble off stage.

"It wasn't that bad," my older sister Mariam said, giving me a hug and handing me a linty throat lozenge she'd dug out of her sweater pocket.

"It was a disaster," Hope half-shouted, pacing up and down the hall that led to our meager dressing room. She sent me a wrathful look. "Why couldn't you have just stuck to the plan? You ruined everything."

"It was two seconds," Micah said, folding his arms across his chest and glaring at Hope. "Nobody even noticed. And her voice sounded amazing before it died. That sound is something else, Adie …"

"You *would* say that," Hope snapped, "you always take her side no matter what stupid stunt she pulls."

"That's not—"

"It might not have been the most ideal time to test out something new," my dad interrupted quietly, squeezing my shoulder gently as he passed by. He smiled faintly but didn't look at me. "We can talk about it later when we get home."

I looked at him anxiously as he passed, taking in his weary expression and the tired lines on his face. He looked exhausted. And disappointed.

"Are you okay?" my mom asked anxiously, peering into my face. "Does it hurt?"

"I'm fine." It came out a rasp and the pain was so sharp that I involuntarily covered my throat with my hand.

"Oh dear," she said, "we'll go to the doctor first thing tomorrow. No more talking for you, young lady. We'll take you right home and get you some hot lemon and honey."

"We can't go home now," Hope protested. "I want to see the rest of the show."

"Your sister's health comes first," my mom said, a warning note in her voice.

"Oh right, I forgot. Princess Adeline always comes first—"

"Hey, don't talk about her like that," Grady said, glaring at Hope furiously.

"It's fine," I said, trying not to wince. I laid a reassuring hand on Grady's shoulder. "We don't need to go home. I'm just going to get a drink and—"

"I'll take care of her," Phil said smoothly, appearing beside me and handing me one of those squeezy apple juice containers that little kids use.

My skin prickled when his clammy fingers brushed against mine and I took the juice from him quickly and stepped away. He had a smile on his face, but I could feel the anger bristling inside of him. He was nearly always angry, but this time I could see his clenched hands shaking at his sides. He also had a heavy-looking green canvas bag over his shoulder that I'd never seen before.

The juice was nice and cold on my throat, and I closed my eyes both in relief and to shut out the reality of what I had done. What had I been thinking? The look on my dad's face …

When I opened my eyes again, Grady, Phil, and Hope were the only ones still standing there.

Phil and Hope weren't paying attention to me, they were looking at each other, exchanging one of those long glances like they were sending urgent telepathic messages between them.

I looked away quickly, pretending that I didn't notice.

My parents had tried to teach all of us to be kind and always look for the best in people, but I had disliked our manager Phil from almost the moment I'd met him.

He'd been a member of our old church back when my parents were into this weird, alternative religion thing. He'd been a singer himself once. And he was a good enough manager, I supposed; he had certainly worked hard for us and our careers had blossomed from almost the second he'd come on board.

But he was also one of those old-school guys who thought that children, and especially girls, should be seen and not heard, who should do what they were told without arguing, and who should look pretty and smile and shut up.

Besides his awful personality, he was old and losing his hair. I couldn't figure out why on earth my beautiful, talented sister would ever be interested in somebody like him. Even though she was bossy and bad tempered sometimes, I thought she could still do so much better than gross Phil.

As far as I knew, I was the only one who had found out they were even seeing each other. At least none of the other kids had said anything, although it was a little hard to miss. My parents would have been furious if they'd known, and I'd nearly told them many times when Hope was being extra annoying.

I hadn't felt right about keeping a secret that big from my parents, but Hope was old enough to make her own decisions. She'd begged me not to tell when I'd caught them sneaking a kiss outside our dressing room last year. She was twenty-two years old, so it wasn't like she was underaged or anything. But still, she could do so much better than greasy Phil.

"You two did a great job tonight," he said, beaming at Hope, and then down at Grady. "The whole thing was *almost* right on target. The crowd was with you the whole time. At least for the most part."

He shot me a sideways glance and I knew that even though he was smiling on the outside, inside he was fuming.

Beside me, I felt Grady tense up and he looked up at Phil with undisguised anger.

Phil was usually careful never to criticize any of us too badly in front of our parents. And when he did say stuff in front of them, he made out like he was just looking out for us and was being hard on us for the sake of our career. He saved his worst lectures for when he had us alone.

"All right, you two, run along," he said, making shooing motions at Hope and Grady, "you don't want to miss the rest of the show. I need to talk to your sister."

Hope swung away instantly, but Grady just stood there, looking at me uncertainly.

"It's okay Grady," I said, "we'll only be a few minutes."

He was only thirteen years old, but he'd started getting more and more surly and argumentative with everyone, especially Hope and Phil. I didn't want him getting in trouble when it was me who'd genuinely messed up.

Phil waited until the door was firmly shut behind him before he reached over and grabbed my arm, giving it a sharp tug.

"Emergency meeting," he said coldly to me, his smile dropping away. "Now."

"Ow," I said, pulling away and rubbing my arm. "Look, I know I messed up, but can't we do this tomorrow? I'm really tired and my throat hurts."

"Well, that's your own fault, isn't it? If you had have listened to me and just blended in with everyone else, then we wouldn't be having this conversation. But, since you seem intent on ruining your sister's, I mean your entire family's, career, I think this is a discussion that we need to have. Now."

I groaned inwardly and followed Phil down the hallway,

wanting to get this lecture over as fast as possible. But to my surprise, he led me deeper into the building and then up one narrow flight of stairs and then another. The heavy bag on his shoulder scraped against the wall and I eyed it suspiciously, wondering what he was up to.

"Where are we going?" I asked, my voice coming out a raspy whisper. All I wanted was to get changed, go back, and watch the rest of the show and forget this night had ever happened.

"I wanted to go somewhere extra private where we could have a little chat," he said, slamming open a metal door at the top of the stairs and ushering me past him.

The cold hit me as soon as I stepped outside and I sucked in my breath and rubbed my arms. I was only wearing the thin dress I'd worn on stage. We were on the roof of the building, the whole city spread out before me in glittering lights. It was beautiful but also freezing.

"W ... why are we here?" I asked, my teeth already chattering. I jumped and spun around as the heavy metal door slammed shut. For a second I panicked, thinking that he'd left me up there to die. But when I saw the expression on his face, I sort of wished he *had* left me up there alone. He looked downright murderous.

"That was a nice little stunt you pulled out there," Phil said coldly. He dropped the duffle bag he'd been carrying onto the snowy roof with a heavy thud. "You know you nearly ruined the show?"

"I'm sorry," I said, quickly backing up a step. "I know I messed up. It just seemed so right. I wasn't trying to—"

"No, clearly you weren't trying at all. Even when I tried to impress on you the importance of blending in and not show-casing your disability."

"Disability? I'm not ... Micah said he liked the way I sounded."

"Well, Micah always tries to see the best in everyone, doesn't he? They all humor you and treat you like a spoiled princess while you slowly drag this group to the ground. I have warned you time and time again to just follow the program. I have an extremely specific niche for your group, and it will be impossible to market you at all anymore if you insist on ruining everything."

"I don't think I'm—"

"No, you don't think at all, do you? You don't even consider the consequences of your actions on everyone else. It's not just *your* career on the line. What do you think is going to happen to your precious family if people stop paying to see you sing?"

"That ... that wouldn't happen. Our fans love—"

"They *used* to. But they're dropping like flies thanks to you. I have a bag full of hate mail and rejection letters that tells a very grim story."

"What? What are you talking about?"

I glanced down at the bag and saw that the zipper had split open and inside were piles of handwritten envelopes and scattered pieces of paper.

"Go on, look at it. Those are actual letters with stamps that people had to pay postage for just so they could write to tell us that they're not fans anymore. And the rest are copies of all the emails I printed off. Not just fans you've lost, but all the bookings that you've messed up for us, too."

"We haven't lost bookings, have we?" I asked, feeling a stab of alarm.

"Do you know how difficult you've made my job? I practically have to beg venues to take you now. They expect a certain sound, Adeline, and *you* are not it anymore."

I stared at him in shock, my thoughts churning slowly like mud.

"Your parents didn't want me to show these to you; they thought you'd been through so much. Poor Adeline. She's so precious that she can't bear to hear the hard truth. They wanted to support you no matter how much you were bringing the family down."

"That ... that's not true?" The words came out a question and I kept my arms wrapped protectively around my shivering body, wanting to be anywhere but in this horrible nightmare.

"I didn't want to do this, Adie. But you left me no choice. You wouldn't listen to me. You always want to do things your own way no matter how much it hurts anyone else.

"It's not just your voice, it's your entire disrespectful attitude. And you've infected the other children with it, too. You've become too unruly, and the younger children are following your lead. Grady is almost out of control and Flora is not far behind him. That is entirely your fault. You're selfish, Adeline, there's no other way to put it."

Anger flared up through all the hurt and confusion. If there was one thing I knew about myself, it was that I wasn't selfish. I would do anything to help my family.

"No," I said through chattering teeth, glaring at Phil, "that's not true. You're wrong."

"Oh, really? Then prove it. You're all talk about how family comes first, but then you go ahead and pull a stupid stunt like you did tonight without giving them a second thought. Do you have any idea how competitive this industry is? One little slip-up like this can cost you years to recover. But you're too much of an entitled, spoiled brat to think of anyone but yourself. Read the letters if you don't believe me, Adeline."

I stared down at the papers with a sudden fear growing in my belly. I didn't want to look. I didn't even want to go near them. I backed away a step and stumbled, my numb feet sliding in the snow.

"I want to go inside," I said, tears stinging my eyes. I wiped them away stiffly.

"You want to run away because you know I'm telling the truth and you can't face it. Fine, if you won't read them then I will." He grabbed what looked to be a handwritten letter from the top of the stack.

"I have been a faithful fan for the last ten years. I won't be listening to you anymore. Your music has changed, and the quality is not the same since your daughter's voice was damaged. I think she needs to move on to a different career.

"Here's another one. The band is great, but there are too many singers. Adeline does not fit in with the overall look and sound. We will not be booking you in the future."

I looked at him, stunned.

"Do you hear me, Adie? There are actual venues that are turning your family away because of you. And not just one venue, but dozens of them. You are dragging everyone down."

"No," The reality of his words suddenly hit me, and I knelt down beside the bag and sifted through the sheets of paper with trembling fingers. The whole bag was stuffed full of them. How could this many people hate *me*? How could this many people really think I was holding my family back?

I started to cry. I hadn't cried since the fire, not through my painful recovery or all the ups and downs that followed, but now I broke down in great, gulping sobs that threatened to pull me apart.

"Now, you see what I've been trying to tell you," Phil said, piling all the papers back into the bag and zipping it shut. He hefted it back to his shoulder and stood there staring down at me coldly like I was an insect he was about to crush.

"All right, get up, that's enough. I only showed you for your own good so you can make better choices in the future. I just don't think you're a good fit for this business anymore, and the sooner you see it the better it is for everyone."

His words flew at me like daggers and buried themselves in my chest, making me cry even harder.

"Okay, Adeline, I said that's enough. We need to get back downstairs. Your family will start wondering where we are, and I want to keep this conversation between us. Pull yourself together."

But I couldn't. I could only sit there in a shivering, sobbing heap.

"I said get up, you spoiled little—"

I gasped as he grabbed me roughly by the arm and tried to yank me upright.

"Hey, what's going on here?"

Phil let me go so abruptly that I sat down hard on the snowy roof with a yelp.

I looked up to see a figure coming out of the darkness like an avenging angel. I'd only met her a few times and I'd never spoken to her. I'd mostly seen her smiling and laughing in television interviews or singing on stage. She wasn't smiling now, though. She looked downright lethal.

"Oh, hey, um, Angelika," Phil said, his voice rising into a frightened squeak. He flashed his full-toothed smile at her and backed a few steps away from me hastily, giving a nervous little laugh that sounded like a braying mule. *He he he he he.* "She's just having a bit of a drama moment. You know teenagers."

Angelika narrowed her eyes at him and took a step closer.

"Are you all right?" she said, switching her gaze to me. "Did he hurt you?"

"Of course not," Phil said, his voice taking on that fake-jolly Uncle tone he used with the younger kids. "Adie and I are old friends. I was just trying to help her."

"That's not what it looked like to me," Angelika said, not taking her eyes off me. "Did he hurt you?"

"Um, no," I said, sniffling. My arm stung from where he'd grabbed me and there was a gaping wound somewhere inside my heart that was still bleeding, but she didn't need to know about all that. "I'm okay."

Your family would be better off without you. You're dragging them down.

The words swirled around inside me and I glanced over at the edge of the rooftop wondering why I'd been spared in the fire in the first place if I was such a burden to them.

"She's fine," Phil said impatiently. "Let's go, Adeline. That's enough of the hysterics."

He reached out toward me again and I shrank back instinctively, not wanting him anywhere near me.

"Leave her alone," Angelika said coldly. "I think you've done enough for tonight. I'll look after her."

"Oh, that's not necessary." Phil looked at her in real alarm, his bulgy eyes flicking at me and then back to her. Despite the cold, a sheen of sweat burst out on his forehead. "This is family business. You don't have to worry about—"

"Go away," she interrupted sharply, rolling her eyes in exasperation as he scuttled reluctantly toward the door. "God, is he always like that?"

"Yes," I whispered as soon as the door had closed safely behind him. "But he's done a lot for our family so we're grateful for his help."

She raised an eyebrow at me, and I looked away, staring again at the sparkling city below us.

"Well, don't give him too much power. It's you guys who do most of the real work, right?"

"Yes, but—"

"No buts. I've only met the man for two seconds, but I can already tell you'd be better off without him. I hate arrogant control freaks like that."

I gaped at her. Everyone always said how lucky we were to have Phil managing our career. We'd only become popular after he'd come on board and changed things to make us more mainstream.

"Why are you out here without a coat?" she asked me, shrugging out of her own plush, velvety black coat and sliding it over my shoulders.

"Oh, don't," I protested. "I'm okay. Don't worry about me. You have to get ready for your concert."

"I'm as ready as I'll ever be," she said. Her arms were bare like mine had been, but she didn't seem to be feeling the cold. "I like having time to think by myself before I go on. You should get inside, though. You're freezing. What on earth were you doing up here anyway?"

For a long moment, I couldn't say anything.

"Phil was just reminding me how badly I messed up tonight," I said finally, gulping. "It was so awful. I ruined everything. I never think before I act."

"Oh, it probably wasn't as bad as you think," she said with a laugh. "You wouldn't believe how many times I've messed up. In all sorts of ways. People will forget all about it over time, if they ever even noticed in the first place. We can't be perfect all the time."

"I know, but this is different. My family has done so much for me. My voice … me … I'm messing up all these opportunities for them. I can't—"

My voice broke again, making me choke. I felt like I'd eaten broken glass, but I couldn't stop talking.

"I'm just so tired of this," I said wearily. "Sometimes I just want to go back to the farm and be a normal kid again."

"Did you live on a farm?" Angelika asked curiously.

"Yeah, before the fire. We still own it and everything, but the house is rented out to some friends of my parents while it's being fixed up. So, we can't go back. We had a pony, but he passed away a couple of years ago. I used to love riding."

"Horses are wonderful. My boyfriend owns some thorough-breds, or at least he owns shares in them. And my sister works on a horse farm on Vancouver Island."

"She does?" I said, wiping my eyes and trying to not sniffle into Angelika's expensive-looking coat.

"Yep, she loves it. Eddie is sending a bunch of his retired racehorses there so they can be trained for new careers. I'm hoping to learn how to ride this summer when I go and visit. It's all new and exciting."

"It sounds nice," I said. "Thank you so much for talking to me. I don't want to take up anymore of your time, though. I know you have a show to do."

"Oh, it's no trouble at all. I like a bit of distraction from my nerves."

"You get nervous?" I said in disbelief. That was one thing that no one in my family ever had to worry about. All us kids had been on stage since we were in diapers, so we pretty much felt comfortable in front of any audience.

"Yep, all the time. I used to have to throw up every night before I went on. Thankfully, that doesn't happen too much anymore. We should get you inside, though. Do you have something warm to change into?"

I hadn't realized quite how cold I was until I stood up and discovered that my arms and legs were half-frozen and not working properly. To my mortification, Angelika had to help me down the stairs to keep me from falling and lead me back to our dressing room.

I felt like I was about four years old as my mom thanked her for bringing me back about a million times in gushing tones and the little kids practically hung off her in an effort to get close and say hello. It was horribly embarrassing.

"Thanks again," I told Angelika as I gave her back her coat, but she waved me off.

"Don't mention it," she said over her shoulder as she swept away. "Maybe I'll see you around."

There was no sign of Phil or Hope, which was something to be grateful for. I couldn't stop shivering, though. Even once I was in warm clothes and had a hot drink in my hands.

My mom fussed over me a little bit, but she was distracted by trying to herd the younger kids into order so they could watch the rest of the concert quietly from backstage without bothering anyone or knocking anything over.

I watched the rest of the concert with everyone else, but in my head I was miles away. I couldn't stop thinking about the awful thing Phil had said. And all those letters ….

That night I lay in bed, tossing and turning and feeling sick. Not able to stop thinking about what had happened.

I hate Phil, I thought, startling myself with the realization. I had never hated anyone before. *But that doesn't mean he's wrong about this. Maybe I have been selfish. I probably am holding my family back. I'm sure Dad thinks that too.*

But the next morning, the immediate decision of what to do was made for me when I woke up with a terrible cold and a raging fever. I stayed in bed that day while everyone else went off to the library to do schoolwork. I just lay there getting sicker and sicker until I could hardly see straight.

My throat burned and nothing made it feel any better, which seemed fitting because I was still full of guilt, and part of me was convinced that this was my punishment for messing up so badly on stage.

I was sick for over a week, and at the end I was left barely able to speak at all.

We finally had to go to the doctor, who took one look at me and referred me to a throat specialist who had a wait list two months long.

"I'm so sorry this happened to you, Adeline," my mom said tearfully, "after all you've been through, too."

From my spot on the couch, I could see Hope in the kitchen stirring a pot of noodles. At my mother's words a small, secretive smile tugged at her lips and she began to hum something under her breath.

Hope doesn't like me at all, I thought in surprise, wondering how I'd never seen that before. An uneasy feeling crawled through my stomach. *How long has she felt that way?*

My family had two smaller bookings organized for the next week, and it was clear that I would not be going along with them. Even listening to them practice was agony, and I mostly stayed in my room pretending to do schoolwork and really just miserably staring at the ceiling.

The first gig was a lunchtime one at a local hall. I spent the day doing house chores and trying to come to terms with the fact that this might be the rest of my life. I would be stuck at home forever like Cinderella and never get to sing again.

I had dinner ready when they got home and pretended to smile while my youngest sister Flora hung off my arm and excitedly told me everything that had happened that day in painful detail so I wouldn't feel left out.

"And someone called to talk about Adie," Mariam interrupted, arching her eyebrows at me. "Mom won't tell us who it was but she talked to them for a *long* time."

"Maybe it was a boyfriend," Flora said, giggling.

"Ooooh," the twins sang in a sing-song chorus.

"I bet it was a talent scout," Grady said loyally.

Hope snorted and rolled her eyes, turning quickly away before my parents could reprimand her.

"The call was for your *sister*," my mom said firmly, shaking her head to try and shut them all up. "I will tell her first in private."

And that set them off again on another round of non-stop guessing about who my secret caller could be.

Mom caught me later that night just as I was heading into the bathroom to have a shower. In our cramped apartment, where we were all crammed three to a room and practically lived on top of one another, the two miniscule bathrooms were pretty much the only places where you could be alone or have a heart-to-heart conversation. And even then, you had to keep your voice down because the walls were so thin. The only other option was sneaking out on the rickety fire escape that overlooked the alley behind the building. Something we only did when our parents weren't around.

"Adie," Mom whispered, shutting the door firmly behind her. "You'll never guess who called."

Her eyes were bright with excitement and I could tell she was dying to share this secret with me. But for some reason all I felt was a gnawing dread.

"No guesses?" she asked, nudging me a little.

"Nope." I shook my head. "I give up."

"Oh, you're no fun. It was *Angelika*." She clasped her hands together, sounding thrilled. "She was calling to check up on you. You must have made quite the impression on her. Did you know that her sister, Bree, works on a farm for retraining racehorses? Her sister likes horses just like you do. Isn't that a nice coincidence? She writes a blog about the farm."

"Yeah, Angelika told me about that when we were out on the ... I mean, when I met her at the concert."

"It has a funny name—October Horses. Did she happen to mention that they take on working students to come live there and work with the horses?"

"No," I said, suddenly feeling cold all over. I knew exactly where this conversation was headed now. "She didn't."

There was a long silence that neither of us seemed to want to break. Mom's expression fell a little, and she reached out and gently squeezed my hand.

I knew then that on the other side of that silence my entire life would change forever. It would mean that I was out of the group, that I wasn't going on tour with my family. That they'd be moving on. Without me ....

My mom was the first to speak.

"Angelika reached out during her busy schedule to hand you this opportunity, sweetheart. She didn't have to do that. I think you should consider it. Strongly."

She cleared her throat a few times and looked down at the

floor before meeting my gaze again. "Our tour is coming up so fast and we're not going to be able to even see the voice therapist before we go. I honestly don't think you're going to be able to sing for a while—"

"You don't want me to come with you," I said flatly, pulling away. I knew I was being childish. But the hurt I felt cut through me like a dull knife, leaving my heart split wide open. I wanted to crawl away into a dark hole and hide. We'd looked forward to this tour for so long. We'd bought an old bus and had converted it to have sleeping bunks and a full bathroom. It was going to be a huge adventure. I couldn't imagine for one second not being a part of it.

"Adeline, you know that's not true," she said firmly, switching to her no-nonsense mom voice. "I always want my kids around me. All of them. But I have the feeling that this tour wouldn't be the best thing for you. Phil says—"

"Phil." I practically spat the name out. "I couldn't care less what Phil thinks. He doesn't care about me. He doesn't care about any of us besides Hope. Not really. He just wants a paycheque."

I clapped a hand over my mouth and looked at her in alarm. I had never said anything like that to my mom about anyone. It was practically a sin in our house not to speak kindly of other people. Only Hope broke the rules on that one.

My mom inhaled sharply and then let all the air out through her nose, something she did when she was forcing herself to be patient with us.

"Some of what you say might be true, but I think you need some time alone to reflect on your angry words," she said with an annoying level of calm.

"Phil isn't out to get you, and nobody wants to leave you behind. But don't you think you deserve more than to just be a backstage helper on this tour, Adie? You'd end up hating it by the end of the year. Your father agrees with me that you need to take a break to really heal properly. If you're on tour with us there will be a lot of temptation for you to push yourself to sing again before you're ready."

She stood up and pushed a piece of paper into my hands.

I looked down and saw a phone number scrawled on it in my mom's handwriting.

"Maybe this is a sign that a singing career isn't meant to be for you. At least not now. Maybe this is your chance to try something else."

She paused, meeting my horrified gaze with sympathy in her eyes. "The decision is yours, but I think this is an opportunity you shouldn't miss. Promise that you'll think carefully about it."

"Fine, I'll think about it," I muttered ungratefully as the door shut gently behind her.

I looked down at the paper in my hands with hot, dry eyes, scarcely able to breathe.

It took me three days to work up the courage to make the call. I waited for a day when my entire family was out practicing at the studio. We were allowed to use a small space for free at the music store where Micah and my dad worked. Which was lucky because we couldn't really practice at home anymore without the neighbours complaining about the noise.

I didn't have my own cell phone since a plan for ten people was out of our budget, so I was stuck waiting until I was finally alone to use the land line in the living room.

I took a deep breath, wiping my sweating palms on my pants and dialed with shaking fingers. I could hear my heart hammering away in my chest.

"Hello?" a man's voice said loudly when the call connected.

I gulped, wondering if I'd dialed the wrong number somehow.

"Um. I'm, um, looking for Angelika. I'm, ah, Adeline …"

"Hang on." The phone knocked against something sharply,

making me wince. There was a murmur of voices in the background.

"Oh, my gosh, Adeline," a familiar voice said a second later. "It's so good to hear from you. I'm glad you're okay. I was worried there."

"You were worried about me?" I asked in confusion.

"Yes, look, so here's the scoop," she said, like we were old friends conspiring together about something exciting. "I asked my sister and the farm owners if you could intern at October Horses for the year and they said yes."

"Um, you did? They did?" I asked in disbelief. "But they don't even know me. Isn't there like an application to fill out or something?"

"Oh, don't worry about that. They're excited to have you. So, it's settled then? You'll go?"

"I—" I began, my voice cracking painfully in the way it did sometimes now when I was stressed out. Everything was happening way faster than I'd meant it to.

But it was the sound of my own voice that actually made the decision for me. There wasn't any point going on tour while I sounded like that. It would be months of hanging around uselessly while Hope and sweaty Phil glowered at me like I was some sort of parasite.

"Yes, I'll go to the farm," I said, forcing enthusiasm into my voice. "And thank you. You didn't have to do any of this."

"I know. I wanted to. I guess I see a little of myself in you, Adie. It wasn't easy for me when I started out, either. I didn't know anything, and I had to learn how to protect myself as I went along. Which was a painful, confusing process. But there were good people who helped me out. I guess this is my turn to pay it forward."

"Thanks again—" I started to say but she cut me off.

"No worries. I already told them you'd be coming this week-end. I had a feeling you'd say yes. They'll meet you at the bus station so just call and tell them when you're arriving. Oh, and I told them you were already a fan of the farm and followed my sister's blog. So maybe make sure to check them out online before you get there. You did say you could ride, right? I told them that you did. Anyway, I'm sure it will all be fine. Good luck. And have fun."

And before I could say anything else, she'd hung up.

I didn't tell anyone that I was going until a couple of days later. I just couldn't bring myself to say it out loud. It would just feel too real if I did.

It wasn't until my latest showdown with Phil that I sealed my fate. It was a typical dark winter day in the city with two feet of dirty snow sitting heavily on the ground and a cold, wet sleet falling. It was the miserable, nasty type that was not quite rain and not quite snow but managed to freeze and soak you at same time whenever any of us went out.

"Do you think people will still come tonight if the roads are bad?" Mariam said anxiously from her seat near the window.

"They always do," Mom replied automatically, walking by with an armful of laundry. "Now, we need to get all our chores done before we go. We have two hours until Phil comes to pick us up in the van and he'll expect us to be ready. Come on, kids, this laundry won't put itself away."

"I call first shower," Hope said quickly, glancing at the load of laundry in our mom's arms before turning abruptly toward the bathroom.

"Fine, but don't be too long. And don't use up all the hot water. Mariam, you fold and put away. Grady and Adeline, make the sure kitchen is clean and that your younger sisters have their clothes laid out. Your father and Micah will be home from work any second and we want to be ready. Come on, hop to it."

"I'll pay you ten dollars if you do my share of the kitchen

cleaning," Grady said as soon as our mom was out of earshot. He didn't lift his gaze from the comic book he'd hidden in his lap under the table. Our parents didn't like him reading comics or graphic novels and refused to buy them. He didn't bother arguing with them. He, just saved up his meager allowance and bought them secretly himself.

"Nice try," I said, running a cloth under the hot water tap. The whole family had been up late the night before rehearsing so today had been a bit of a lazy day. Lunch dishes still sat in the sink along with bread pans that had been too hot to wash when they'd come out of the oven. "Besides, you don't have any money."

"Yes, but one day I will," he said fiercely, glancing up from his comic book. "One day I'll be rich, and then you and me and Micah can live in a big mansion in the country where nobody bothers us. And you can have a horse again and I'll have dogs. And a garage full of cars. And a motorcycle. And a pool."

"Well, that sounds really nice. And I bet you'll do it, too. You're just the type of person who will become a successful tycoon. But what about everyone else? You just want us three to live there?"

"Well, they can visit sometimes, I guess. But it will be just the three of us all the time."

"Sounds peaceful," I said, laughing and pitching another dish cloth at him. "Counters need doing."

"Yeah, yeah." He rolled the comic up into a thin tube and then stuck it in his back pocket with his shirt down over top of it to keep it hidden.

"You ready for tonight?" I asked him as he started half-heartedly wiping the counters and table. It was a fairly big venue and I was actually happy that I'd been roped in to going along to help. I was sick of being stuck at home. "Are you excited?"

"Meh, I guess so. I'll be more excited when we get to go on

tour, though. I'm sick of this dump. I hope the next place is bigger. I wish we'd never left the farm."

"Me neither," I said honestly. "But hey, success takes sacrifices, right? And it's not all bad. We're all together as a family. That's the important bit."

I broke off suddenly, realizing how little those words meant now that I wouldn't be going with them this time. How on earth was I supposed to tell Grady that I wasn't going with him on tour?

"If you say so," he said darkly, and then he worked in silence, refusing to say another word.

I glanced over to him, feeling a stab of worry. Grady had always been a funny kid. He was fierce and stubborn and before the fire, he'd always been full of laughter and had a wicked, sarcastic sense of humour that kept us all in stitches.

But that had been before the fire. Ever since we'd moved from the farm to the city, he'd changed. He'd become moody and secretive, and he buried himself in his comic books rather than spend time with the rest of us. He still sang and went to rehearsals without complaint, but all the joy seemed to have gone out of it.

He mostly ignored our younger sisters, who had always adored him, and he had become downright surly to my parents and Hope. And lately, he'd practically been openly hostile to Phil.

Mom thought Grady's mood shift was because he'd turned thirteen this year and was becoming a teenager, but I didn't agree. I was closest to him out of all my siblings, and I knew there was something that was eating him up inside.

Hope was still in the shower when we were done. The twins were in the living room playing games on their leapfrog tablet. Grady disappeared somewhere and I went from room to room laying out the clothes everyone would need for that night. It was easier to set out everything we needed early on, otherwise, there would be a mad dash ending in tears at the last minute.

My dad and Micah had been lucky enough to find work at a music shop three or four days a week. They taught lessons and minded the counter and got to hang out with aspiring musicians all day. And that meant that we were all allowed to use their rehearsal space for free.

Mariam worked at the coffee shop downstairs a couple days a week, too. With ten mouths to feed, everyone needed to pitch in. I would have loved to have gotten a job too, but mom wanted me home to focus on my schoolwork and help out with minding the little kids.

Despite trying to be organized, an hour and a half later and our apartment was in chaos. Dad and Micah had come home to try and get ready, leaving everyone else struggling to find enough mirrors to do makeup and hair. This venue wouldn't have a dressing room so everything had to be done ahead of time at home.

The twins were dressed and were excitedly jumping back and forth on the couches singing some annoying song at the top of their lungs.

Flora had missed her nap and she was grumpy and half-asleep.

"Here, Mom," I said, finding her trying to get dressed with Flora hanging off her arm. "I'll take her. You need to get ready."

Flora clung to my neck sleepily as I lifted her up and carried her down the hall toward the bench by the front door.

"I need my bear," she whispered as I wrapped her into her winter coat and stuffed her warm purple boots onto her feet. "He wants to go."

"All right, you stay here, I'll get him."

She immediately curled up on the bench and fell back asleep while I went down the short hallway to the room she shared with me and the twins.

Even in the big farmhouse, we had never been able to have our own rooms, but shoving four people on bunkbeds into these tiny, cramped quarters was a little much, even for us, especially when there was no endless acreage to explore outside.

The room was as tidy as it could be under the circumstances, but it still took me a few minutes to locate the right stuffed animal under the pile of others. He had once been a fancy sort of bear who had been made out of an old fur coat. Most of the fur had worn off now and his glass eyes had been replaced so many times I couldn't remember what the originals had looked like. He'd been my mom's when she was little, and then had been given to Hope and then to me, and I'd passed it to Grady, and now he was Flora's. By now, he was a well-beloved family member even though he looked pretty bedraggled.

I glanced at the clock and swore under my breath. Phil would be knocking on the door at any second. I wanted to avoid being alone with him at all costs.

"Here's your bear," I said, trotting down the hall to find Flora already standing on a chair, working the deadbolt on our door back and forth. She dropped to the floor and flung open the front door with a squeal of excitement.

"Uncle Phil!" she cried, launching herself at him before he'd even stepped inside. He was in no way related to us, but that's what the younger kids had decided to call him for some reason.

"Princess Flora," he said, scooping her up. "The star of the show."

My stomach curdled and I slid out of the way before he could see me. I wondered bitterly how old Flora would be when he'd stop thinking she was cute and turn on her, too. Or maybe it was just me he hated.

"I have my boots on," Flora said. "I'm all ready to go."

"I see that," he said, "but I don't think that princesses wear old boots, kiddo. You should put your nice shoes on. You want to look your best, don't you?"

"Umm," Flora said doubtfully. "But I need to wear boots to keep my feet dry in the snow."

"You can certainly wear them if you want," he said, his voice lowering with disapproval. "I just thought you wanted to be a star. Stars shine all the time, Flora, or people stop watching them. Now, do you think those ugly old boots make you look like a shining star or are there some sparkly shoes that would make you look like a pretty princess?"

I froze in place, my breath caught in my throat, and then that old familiar rage swept over me like a river, washing my need to avoid Phil right out the window.

"That's enough," I said, marching into the hallway, "you leave her alone."

I scooped a bewildered Flora out of his arms and clung to her like she was a life-preserver.

"She is five years old. She needs to wear boots so her feet stay warm and dry, so she doesn't get sick. And she doesn't need to hear any of that sexist crap out of you, either. She is a little girl."

A flash of anger crossed his face and he clenched his jaw. Then he smoothed his expression and sent me an insincere smile.

"Well, hello again, Adeline," he said loudly, in his jovial-uncle voice. His glance flicked over my shoulder and when he saw the three of us were still alone, he narrowed his eyes at me. "Such a ray of sunshine as always, I see. I spoke to your parents last night and they mentioned that you might just have come to your senses and won't be going on tour with us. Such a wise girl. I've been praying and praying that you find your place in this world. Going to be cleaning out some horse stables, was it?"

He smiled at me nastily and I wondered how on earth my parents couldn't see what a terrible person he was.

"I have a place," I said firmly. "Here with my family."

"You're squeezing me too tight," Flora said, squirming until I set her on the floor. She kicked off her boots and stood there scowling down at them.

"Right, right, of course," Phil said smoothly, "you're all about family. And I'm sure you'd make a nice little backstage helper on the tour if you could keep your mouth shut for more than two seconds and stop arguing whenever anyone tells you what to do."

I gasped and took a step back, hardly able to believe that he was talking like that in front of Flora.

She was looking up at us uncertainly, taking in everything and my heart sank. How was I just supposed to go away and leave them all for a year? Who was going to stand up for them when Phil started treating the younger kids like he treated me? I couldn't just abandon them.

Suddenly Mom appeared beside me, squeezing my arm gently and smiling down at Flora.

"Are we almost ready to go here?" she asked, oblivious to the tension in the air.

"Just about," Phil said, "Adeline was just sharing her good news."

"Oh?" My mom looked at me and clasped her hands together. "Oh, I knew you'd decide to go. I'm so happy for you, darling. It's going to be the best move for you. I'm so relieved that you made the call to Angelika I know you won't regret it."

I could only stand there mutely, nodding my head as if in agreement. Feeling the weight of Phil's malicious gaze upon me.

"I'm so proud of you," my mom said, putting a firm hand on my shoulder. "I think this will be so good for you. I honestly wonder if we didn't do you kids a disservice focusing so hard on the music all the time. I think sometimes you missed out on other opportunities."

The warmth in her voice made me look up and meet her gaze, and I could see her pouring all her love into me in that way she did with all of us when she had the time. When she wasn't too busy to remember we existed.

"Adie's not coming on tour?" Flora asked in confusion.

"She's just going on a little vacation Flora, now put your boots on. You'll catch your death of cold out there if you wear your shoes. I'll bring them along with us. Kids, come on. Phil is here and we're just about to leave."

"What do you mean, Adie's not coming on tour?" Grady said, appearing behind me.

I just shook my head and he looked an me with an incredulous expression that quickly turned to hurt.

"Mom will explain it to you," I said, quickly. I threw on my coat and ducked past Phil to escape into the hallway. I had the feeling it was going to be a long night.

In fact, it was going to be a long year. My fate was sealed and there was nothing to do but see it through to the bitter end.

CHAPTER 9

BREE

I really hope it's okay that I left Adie alone, I thought guiltily, hurrying down to the barn through the snow. *Maybe I should have asked her to come with me.*

My guilt over leaving our new houseguest faded away as the ideas for my blog began swirling around in my head again. I loved this part of being a writer, there was something magical about it when the inspiration hit me full force.

I had a thermos full of coffee, two mugs, and some snacks packed into a shoulder bag. I rehearsed my questions silently again, trying to remember everything I wanted to ask Nancy.

Over the winter, I had been doing my best to release a new blog piece every two weeks or so. In between them, I would just update our social media accounts with photos of the horses now and then.

It seemed to keep our followers happy. But lately, I'd been finding it hard to think up interesting things to write. I wasn't actively dying at the moment, the racehorses hadn't arrived, and we couldn't do much more than trail ride right then.

So, there wasn't really anything new to share. There were only so many pictures of the same trails that people wanted to see.

And the horses were fluffy with winter coats and were not the sleek, beautiful things that our followers had come to love.

I was quite sure my hatred of all things winter was bleeding through into my writing too and was making everything sound a little depressing.

It had been Julie's idea to do some spotlights on the senior horses that lived on the farm while we waited for the new race-horses to arrive.

Last time I'd written an article on Bear. I'd tracked down his old racing history and Lorne had dug up some ancient photos of him from when he was young on the track.

There was a whole spread of pictures of him competing with Lorne and Gretta when he was in his prime. And I'd added some recent shots of him that I'd taken that past fall where he was looking extra handsome. His black coat sprinkled with frosty white hairs stood out against his red plaid jacket and he looked out at the camera with a bold expression.

People had loved it and Bear had become the new instant star of the farm.

So now I had no choice but to keep going with the series. For my second horse, I'd chosen Slate, the big white mare. Her owner Nancy travelled around the world for work doing something or another, and only came home every few months. She hadn't been home over Christmas and until last week, I'd never even met her the entire time I'd been at the farm.

It had always felt weird to me that Nancy and the other owners of the senior horses paid full board for animals that they barely visited. They even paid extra so that Julie would keep the horses brushed and switch out their many blankets whenever the temperature changed.

I'd sort of had it in my head that I wouldn't like Nancy since it felt like she'd abandoned Slate here when the retired show jumper couldn't perform anymore. But it turned out that I'd liked her quite a bit when I'd met her the week before. And it was clear that Slate adored her.

Slate was always a nice, quiet horse to work with, but when Nancy was around, she sort of lit up inside. She arched her neck and nickered under her breath and couldn't stop reaching out with her soft nose to touch Nancy's arm or face or side as if she was reassuring herself every second that her owner was still there.

Snow crunched under my feet as I headed to the barn, humming a little under my breath. The sun was out, and I felt lighter than I had in a while. Talking to my dad a few nights ago had cheered me up more than I'd expected. It had been a weight off my shoulders to finally make the call to see my specialist, too. Even though I couldn't get an appointment for weeks it still felt nice to have actually planned to go.

"Hello," I called, rolling the barn door back a little further. It had melted enough by lunchtime that Julie had turned all the horses out after Chloe and I had left to pick up Adie. So the barn was quiet except the sound of low murmuring down at the far end.

"Hi. Nancy?"

"Hey Bree," she called, sticking her head out into the aisle and giving me a wave. "We're in here. I didn't bother putting her in the cross-ties."

"Thank you so much for doing this," I said. "I brought coffee and snacks."

"Oh, you don't have to bribe me," she said laughing, "but I never say no to snacks."

She took the mug of coffee I handed her and inhaled the aroma deeply before taking a sip.

"I've read your blog, Bree. You're a really good writer, you know. Are you going to pursue that as a career?"

"Oh, I don't know," I said, startled by the question. "I haven't really given the future too much thought, honestly. It's enough of a struggle just trying to handle this winter."

I broke off, blushing, suddenly afraid that I'd shared too much. I hated looking weak in front of strangers. Pity and sympathy were so hard to take.

But Nancy just threw her head back and laughed.

"Winter with horses is definitely not something I miss," she said, grinning at me. "That is the one perk of boarding them out. Have the waters frozen yet?"

"Oh my gosh, yes, we had to bucket water to the horses for weeks. It was awful. I think I pulled my arms half out of their sockets. I never want to see another bucket again."

"Then you'll forget all about it over the summer until it happens again next year. I remember those days well. I was a barn rat for years, so I've done my share of dirty work."

"You were a groom, right? That's how you met Slate."

"Yes, I was a groom, among other things. I worked my way up from my local riding stable to a few different barns around the country. Finally, I got a good break and landed at a really fancy show jumping barn."

She took a sip of coffee while I pulled out my pad of paper and hurriedly scribbled down her words furiously, trying not to miss anything.

"It was a fabulous barn, and they gave me so many opportunities to travel, meet interesting people, and handle world-class horses. I'd been there two or three years before they purchased Slate. And I was lucky enough that she was put under my charge.

"I have to say that it was love at first sight. I didn't care that she was a super-star. She was just so wise and kind and easy to handle. She and her rider competed all over North America and we even travelled overseas to Europe a few times. I loved being there for her. We all worked as a team to get both horses and riders into the ring and onto the podium.

"I was always so anxious that something bad would happen when we flew the horses overseas and back. But ironically enough, we were heading home from a local show when the accident happened.

"It was a big show and had a good selection of classes for younger horses, so we'd brought along a few youngsters that we didn't regularly compete on.

"One of them was a really young, nervous prospect. I don't even know why we bothered to compete him then. He was one of those guys who probably needed to be turned out for a year just to grow up and chill out. Everything scared him and he wasn't interested in trusting me or becoming friends, no matter how hard I tried.

"He was awful in the trailer. He would be fine for a while, and then suddenly just have a melt-down and flail around. That's why I was travelling in the back of the trailer with the horses when the semi-truck smashed into us and flipped the entire rig over."

"Oh, my gosh, I didn't know that," I said, looking at her in shock. "That's how Slate got her scars?"

"Yes. I got off with only a broken arm and some bruises, but the horses weren't so lucky. The gelding and another horse had to be put down on the spot. It was horrible. We'd all loved those horses, so it was devastating for the whole team. And Slate had been badly injured. They weren't even sure at first if she was going to make it.

"When she came home from the veterinary hospital, she was given a year to heal, to see how much things would improve. But it became obvious really early on that she would never be the same.

"I was still living at the barn, doing light jobs while I healed.

There was no health insurance or workers compensation for me back then. But I guess they felt bad because they let me stay on even though I couldn't do much of anything for a while.

"Slate was given the best of care and the best chance to recover. She had good food and turnout, and had massage, and a chiropractor and pulse therapy done every week."

"Well, that was nice of them," I said, surprised. I had assumed they would have dumped her right away as soon as she couldn't perform.

"Oh, yes, they were good people. The plan was to make her comfortable enough to use as a broodmare. Her bloodlines are amazing, so it made sense. But then it turned out that she was infertile; she would never be able to have foals. And then it was time for some hard decisions."

Ah, I thought, *here it comes. Why does money, or lack of money, have to affect everything?*

"I can't really blame them from a practical perspective. I mean, in the short term she was going to need a lot of care just to stay pasture sound. And there was a chance that maybe she wouldn't even be ridable at all in the future. It didn't make sense to pour all that money and time into her if she was just going to be a lawn ornament.

"But something inside of me just couldn't bear to have her be put down. She was always so kind and wise, and I would spend hours out in the field with her just hanging out and talking to her. Having time off from work to heal had given me a chance to think about my future plans, too. Every day I would go out and tell her all about my secret ideas and hopes for the future.

"We'd spent so much time together over the years, and I'd seen what a brave, generous horse she'd been. She'd given us everything of herself, never holding back even when she was tired or sore. She always tried her best. I felt like we owed her that chance.

"One day when the vet was there, I asked him point-blank

what her odds were of ever being comfortably sound enough to ride again. He gave her a sixty percent chance and that was all I needed to hear.

"I had a meeting with my boss and pretty much begged him to make a deal with me. If I could get her sound enough to be a happy trail horse in a year, then they would give her to me. They wanted to make sure she didn't suffer, you see. And I was pretty young at the time, so they wanted to make sure that I was able to keep up with her treatment plan.

"As soon as they agreed, I called my parents and told them that I was moving home and going back to school. I was giving up being a professional groom and going to focus on a different sort of career.

"It was exactly the call they'd been waiting for. They'd been anxiously hoping that I'd get horses out of my system and start being practical.

"They were half right. I was ready to be practical, but I was far from getting horses out of my system.

"I brought Slate home to their small hobby farm, enrolled in school, and got a part time job at night so I could keep up with Slate's massage, chiro, and veterinary treatments. Every night I would massage her healing muscles and hand-walk her as far as she could go.

"And gradually, it worked. By the end of the year Slate and I were able to walk and trot all around the neighbourhood and enjoy exploring our short, local trails. Her old owners sent me her papers and gave her to me on the condition that she would never be sold.

"I finished my first four years of school and realized how much I loved writing. I put my focus on journalism and spent another few years studying and working locally. Slate was getting better and better all that time and we graduated to doing ring work and light dressage. We even showed a few times.

"She has been a fantastic friend. After I met my husband, who is a journalist too, we started travelling and covering world events together. I've seen some amazing sights and have gotten to be a witness to some pivotal historical events. But I'm always happiest when I get to come home and visit my best girl here.

"When my parents finally retired and sold their farm, I moved Slate here to be taken care of. She's not sound enough for riding anymore, but she does enjoy being fussed over and being led on walks down the trail. She's a good girl and I know that Julie takes excellent care of her."

"Wow, that is an amazing story," I said. "Slate is actually my favourite of the seniors after Bear," I told her. "She always has such a sweet expression on her face."

"Yes, she's always been lovely. My dream was to have a small farm of my own and keep her there, but I think we're a few years away from retirement yet. Besides, I love my job and I love helping people. And Slate loves being with the other horses. I'd hate to take that away from her."

"I think you're giving her a great life," I said, suddenly grateful that I'd had this interview with Nancy. I'd sort of been judging her in my head all this time about not coming to visit Slate often. But really, she was a pretty amazing horse person to have gone to the lengths she did to make sure that Slate had a good retirement.

Nancy gave me a quick hug and then led Slate outside into the sunshine so I could take a few pictures of them. My head was buzzing by the time we were done, and I could hardly wait to sit down and get everything put together for my blog.

"Thanks again," I called as I headed back to the house. I glanced at my phone as I quickly headed back up the hill. The interview had taken longer than I'd expected, and I felt another stab of guilt about leaving Adie on her own for so long.

I hope she's doing okay, I thought, *I would hate for her to have a bad first day. I'm a terrible host.*

The house was quiet when I got back in. Julie was probably still in town doing errands and there was no sign of Adie.

I took my boots off and carried them into the living room to set them on their mat by the woodstove. The fire was nearly out so I opened the woodstove door and used the long poker to break up the orange, glowing coals. Then I tossed three more logs on, watching as the fire took and the wood crackled to life.

"Don't worry about getting up, Tom," I told him as he sleepily opened one eye and then closed it firmly again, breaking into a low, rumbling purr.

I climbed the stairs and went right to Adie's door, duty winning over my immediate need to start writing.

"Hey, Adie?" I called through the shut door, knocking lightly. There was no answer.

Maybe she's taking a nap or in the shower or something, I thought, *I don't want to just barge in. I'll check on her in another twenty minutes or so.*

With my host-duty done, I eagerly went to my bedroom and looked down at the pages of notes I'd written, feeling a growing excitement. I quickly plugged my phone into my laptop to upload the new photos and then sat down cross-legged on the bed.

Taking a deep breath, I began to type, setting down the words that were flowing into my brain as fast as I could. I hadn't felt this energized and inspired in a long time.

Sometimes, actually most of the time, writing was hard work for me even though I enjoyed it. But there were times like these when the energy flowed and my fingers felt like they were flying across the keyboard of their own accord. So fast that I could hardly keep up with the ideas and words flowing out of my brain.

I kept going, typing until the sky outside darkened and until Nancy and Slate's story lay fresh and shining on my laptop like a new painting.

I think it sounds even better than the one about Bear and Lorne, I thought, groaning as I sat upright to stretch out my back and flexing my fingers to ease the cramping in my hands. *At least I hope it does.*

That was the weird thing about writing for social media. You had instant feedback on your work. And sometimes, the things you thought were brilliant just fell on dead air and there was almost zero response. And the things you just threw out there with a goofy, ungroomed photo and no editing were the articles that somehow resonated with people. It was always a gamble.

Well, fingers crossed, I thought, making sure to save and carefully back up my work before closing my laptop. I was always cautious to save everything now since that one stormy day when I'd lost a whole day's worth of work in a power outage.

Oh right, I need to check on Adie. I remembered our new guest with a surge of guilt. But when I went back to her room again, there was still no answer to my light knock.

I'll just feed the horses then and catch up with her later. I'm sure she doesn't want me hovering over her.

CHAPTER 10

ADIE

I unpacked as slowly as I could, hanging my clothes reluctantly on their new hangers. The closet was so big that I didn't have nearly enough clothes to fill it. My few things looked a little sad and lonely hanging there at one end.

I was feeling such a swirling mixture of emotions that I could barely breathe. On one hand, my new room was right out of some wonderful story. It was so clean and bright, and I could hardly believe that I didn't have to share it with anyone. But it felt like too much space for just me.

I honestly had given zero thought as to what my life at October Horses would be like. I had only thought about the tour I'd be missing. I'd scarcely cared about what would happen once I actually arrived here.

There was a knock at the door, and I startled, knocking a handful of hangers to the floor with a clatter.

"Um, come in," I said, moving out of the closet and standing awkwardly in the middle of the room.

The door opened and a woman with long, dirty-blonde hair looked in, smiling at me in a kindly way.

I knew right away from the strange scars on one side of her face that this was Julie. I did my best to keep my gaze fixed on her eyes even though I wanted to study the damage done to her. It wasn't nearly as bad as I'd expected. Just a shinier, more pulled area that was not quite right. The skin tugged at the corner of her eye, pulling everything slightly sideways.

"Hey," she said kindly, "I just wanted to introduce myself and see if you wanted to come down and have some hot chocolate by the fire before we go down to the barn. Bree is bringing the horses in from the pasture right now. I'm Julie."

"It's nice to meet you," I said, clearing my throat and moving forward to shake her hand like I'd been taught.

Her grip was warm and firm, and I instantly relaxed, feeling a bit more comfortable here already.

"Come on. I'll show you the rest of the house, although you must be dying to see the barn and the horses first. You had your own horse at home, right?"

"Um," I hesitated, wondering what exactly Angelika had told them about me. "He was a pony. Teddy. And I shared him with my family. We used to ride him everywhere. Even to the store. When we were really young, he'd let us pile as many kids as we could on his back. Sometimes there would be five of us up there."

I broke off, willing myself to stop talking. The horses here were probably a million times fancier than Teddy; they'd probably never carted a pack of laughing kids around bareback or swum in the river or pulled a hand-made cart.

But Julie smiled and nodded. "He sounds like a perfect kid's pony. You know, when I bought my first horse, with my own money that I'd saved up for years and years, I couldn't afford a saddle at first, so I rode bareback everywhere. It was great for developing balance. And also tact; you have to learn to negotiate politely with a horse who can unseat you at the drop of a hat."

I laughed, thinking of how many times we'd slid or jumped or fallen off Teddy. We'd even used him as a diving board into the pond in the summers.

He'd been a real member of the family and we'd all been devastated when he'd died. Nobody had known exactly how old he'd been, but he was probably in his early thirties at least.

"A happy, safe family horse or pony like that is pure gold," Julie went on. "You'll like the senior horses we have retired here. They're all real sweethearts."

"I loved Bree's blog episode on Bear and Lorne," I said, "He looked like such a nice horse. I can't wait to meet them all."

After my last phone call with Angelika, I had made sure to carefully read every single one of the October Horse blog entries that Bree had ever written. I'd even commandeered our old laptop and read the more interesting ones out loud to the younger kids at night.

"Right, well, let's go then and you'll get your tour and I'll show you the lay of the land."

I followed Julie down the stairs, the old floorboards making cracking, squeaking sounds under my feet.

"It's a quirky, old house," Julie said with a laugh. "But we love it."

"Oh, I love old houses, too," I said quickly, "it reminds me a little of our farmhouse back home … I mean back before the fire when we lived on the farm. It's much better than an apartment in the city."

"I have to agree with you there," Julie said, "so this is my bedroom on the right here and there's a bathroom on the left. And here's a little study, or the library as Bree calls it. There are all sorts of interesting books in there so help yourself. And of course, here is the kitchen and you saw the living room when you came in. And here is Lorne."

"Well, hello there," an older man smiled at me from his spot at the kitchen table and beckoned me over. "You must be Adeline.

That's a fine name. My wife Gretta had considered that when she was naming our daughters. It's French, isn't it?"

"Um, yes, it is," I said, a little thrown off by his question. "My mother always wanted to travel to Paris."

"Well, Paris is all right if you like buildings, traffic and trekking around endlessly in museums and galleries and things. It wasn't my cup of tea, but Gretta enjoyed it. I like the country-side much better."

"Oh, so do I," I said, pulling out a chair and sitting down across from him. "It was so weird when we first moved into our apartment. We had to get used to all the constant noises in the building and outside. It's like the city never sleeps, not for a single second. And the buildings crowd in around you wherever you go. There is hardly any space to stretch out and move like in the country. Sometimes it was like I could hardly breathe."

I broke off, embarrassed to have shared so much with someone I'd just met two seconds ago. There was just something about him that made me want to tell the truth.

"That must have been rough on all of you," Julie said, setting down my hot chocolate and giving my shoulder a little squeeze.

"Oh, I'm making it sound worse than it is," I said quickly, "moving there was a decision we all made together. My dad wanted, I mean all of us wanted, to just spend a few years focusing on music and on seeing if we could really forge out a full-time career. It was for the good of the entire family. And at least we were all together. That's the main thing."

I stopped, frowning down at the scarred wooden table in confusion. It hadn't exactly been the entire family that had wanted to leave the farm behind. Grady and Flora hadn't. And, if it really came down to it, neither had I. Although I hadn't said that at the time.

There was an uncomfortable silence.

"Well, why don't you tell me all about your experience with horses," Lorne said kindly.

Haltingly, knowing that my horse background was pitifully small, I told him the same story I'd told Julie about Teddy. Although, now that I was saying it out loud again, it made it sound more like we'd used poor Teddy as transportation and entertainment rather than as a dignified riding pony. I felt my cheeks begin to flush with embarrassment.

Nodding, Lorne pulled a large, leather-bound book across the table and opened it up, rotating it sideways so I could see. It turned out to be a photo album filled with all these fantastic pictures of him and his wife Gretta from when they were young. And filled with horses.

It took me about two seconds to see that my riding and horse handling experience with Teddy was a far cry from what these people must be expecting from me. That photo album was like a window to an entirely different world.

The pictures showed immaculately groomed horses wearing fancy tack with their hair braided and leaping over brightly painted jumps.

Or they wore monogrammed blankets with matching leg wraps, posing regally beside professional-looking grooms.

And I'd never braided a mane or wrapped a leg in my entire life. Teddy had never even *worn* a blanket, not even in the winter. He had his own thick woolly coat to protect him and a little shelter we'd built from scrap lumber that he only chose to use in the worst weather.

I'd never even *watched* a horse show let alone groomed or ridden in one. We barely used the ancient western saddle that had come with Teddy when we'd bought him. It had just sat in a corner gathering dust.

I wondered with a sinking feeling what Angelika had told them about my experience with horses. What were these people expecting me to know how to do? I felt my breathing get shallow, wondering if they'd just kick me out when they discovered that I was there under false pretenses.

Julie must have sensed my discomfort somehow.

"We'll start you off cleaning stalls and helping with feeding until you learn our routine," she said kindly. "And I'll love having some more help in the house. Kids who grow up on farms are always such hard workers. I think you'll fit in just fine around here. Now, if you're done your hot chocolate then let's go meet those horses."

Even though it was only half past five, the sky outside was pitch black and full of stars. The cold air nipped at my cheeks. I pulled my hat down over my ears and followed Julie down the long winding driveway that curved down the hill to the barn.

"We could have driven, of course," she said, "but I like the walk unless the weather is awful."

"I don't mind walking," I assured her quickly. It was true. Even in the city, I'd loved to walk. The motion of it soothed me and straightened my often-wild thoughts out.

From down below, I could hear horses nickering eagerly and buckets being banged and the sound of stall doors rolling open. My heart gave a little leap of excitement.

All farm animals loved dinner time. We'd raised goats and sheep at one point and they'd nearly done cartwheels at night when they knew their grain was coming.

The front door of the barn was wide open and yellow light streamed across the trampled snow.

"Hey, there you are," Bree called, smiling at me warmly, "just in time to help feed. I've brought them in and given them their hay, and now we just need to do grains. Come on, I'll show you the feed room."

The feed room was off to the side and full of neatly labeled tubs and there was a counter full of jars of supplements and bags of cookies. Buckets lined the floor, each one of them neatly labeled, too.

"Wow," I said, looking at all the food. Teddy had gotten to eat plain hay and the occasional carrot and that was it. And he'd had a salt block when we'd remembered to set one out. We hadn't done anything fussy like give him fancy grains. He had been as round as a house as it was.

"We tailor our feeding program to match the needs of each horse," Julie said, coming up behind me. "The boarders are all seniors, some that have underlying medical issues. Ace is a bit of a hard keeper. He's young and still growing so we are constantly trying to keep him from looking too skinny. And Dragon is in full time work when there isn't so much snow. They all have different needs that we have to be aware of."

"Okay," I said, looking at the bewildering array of supplements on the counter.

"All the horses get soaked alfalfa pellets and ground flax that their grains and supplements are mixed with. See, the feed chart is on the wall there. We're going to put a few of the horses under your care once you've settled in, but for now you can just get a feel for the place and help out in a general way."

"Yes," I said quickly when she stared at me expectantly. "I can help out wherever you want me to."

"Perfect, well, how about we take some buckets down to the senior horses. You can take Bear and Slate their food and then we'll introduce you to the whole gang."

Bree smiled as she handed me the two heavy buckets that were steaming with some slimy green mixture. It smelled nice even if it looked completely vile.

The row of horses nickered as we walked by and I smiled as I looked at them, recognizing some of the faces from reading Bree's blog. It was like meeting movie stars in person.

That's Dragon, I thought, edging well away from her as she pinned her ears and tossed her head in my direction. *She's a lot bigger in person. And scarier.*

"Here is Bear," Julie said affectionately, "he's easy to handle. Just ask him to step back out of your space so you can put his food in the bucket. They're all expected to be polite."

The horse looked at me expectantly and I slowly opened his door. He was obviously ancient. The hollows over his eyes were sunken in and his black face had turned nearly white with age. But his eyes were bright and full of intelligence and he looked healthy enough. He was wearing a red plaid coat that stood out boldly against the black of his neck. He gave off the impression of being well-loved, retired royalty.

"Hey, boy," I said softly as he arched his neck and eyed up the bucket in my hands.

Bear nickered eagerly under his breath, the sound coming out a low and musical rumble that echoed in his chest and through his whole body.

"Good boy," I said as he politely stepped back and let me dump his food in the wide tub hanging on the wall.

He plunged his nose into it, dismissing me completely.

"Perfect, the next one is for Slate."

One by one, I met the horses, and Julie let me feed the rest of the seniors. Flicker was a plain brown horse without any white on her who wore a faded green jacket that had clearly been patched a few times. She backed a few feet away while I dumped her food in the tub and then waited for me to leave again before she started to eat. She didn't seem as friendly as Slate and Bear had been.

Next was a little chestnut gelding with a big white blaze and knobbled, boney knees like he'd once been in some sort of accident.

"What happened to him?" I asked Julie, pointing to his knees.

"Oh, just years of hard work, I think. Cooper was a futurity cutting horse when he was quite young and then he competed hard his whole life. It can take a toll on them by the time they reach this age. His whole body is full of arthritis. But he gets around well out on the pasture and he still runs around with his friends. The vet said just to keep him happy and let him live out his life as best he can. He'll tell us when he's had enough."

"Mind yourself around Nipper," Bree said, appearing behind me with a bucket in each hand. "He can be pushy if you're not paying attention to him. Maybe watch me first and then you can do him tomorrow."

There wasn't much to see, though. She just walked into his stall and dumped his bucket of food in the tub. He behaved just as nicely as all the other seniors had.

"Faker," Bree told him, shaking her head. "Don't let him fool you. Sometimes, he'll grab the bucket out of my hand and throw it just for fun. He used to nip me all the time when I wasn't paying attention to him. And you definitely don't want to clean his stall while he's inside. He'll dump your wheelbarrow every single time. Guaranteed."

I looked in at the painted horse who was watching us with a wide-eyed innocent expression. He had a bit of an extra sparkle in his eye though, like he was plotting mischief.

"And this is Ace, of course," she went on, leading us to the next stall. "The best horse who ever lived."

The little bay horse lifted his head from his hay and nickered at her happily. He was quite a bit smaller in real life than he looked online. He was a dark bay with a white star on his head that was barely covered by his scanty forelock. He had a quiet, gentle expression, and he watched Bree with a look of complete adoration. The mirror of the way she was looking at him, actually. It was clear that they were a team.

"You probably read about how he was lame when he first came here," Bree said, running a hand fondly down his neck. "So, we haven't started him back into work yet. He's pasture-sound for sure, and we're just hoping he stays that way once he's under saddle. The vet says he looks great, though. There's no reason he shouldn't be totally fine."

"Bree is an excellent worrier," Julie said, laughing. "He's in perfect shape. Now we just have to wait for this snow to melt so we can have our ring back again."

"Who takes care of Dragon?" I asked a little nervously as the big mare abruptly stuck her head out into the aisle and pinned her ears at nothing I could see.

"Oh boy, don't worry. You won't have to handle her," Bree said. "We flip a coin for it every day and the loser has to feed her."

"She's kidding," Julie said, rolling her eyes. "Dragon is a lot better than when she first came. Having Chloe exercise her has done wonders for her personality. I do hope Chloe can figure out a way to come live here for the summer. We'd love to have her full-time."

"She doesn't live here?" I asked in surprise. Chloe was featured in many of the blog articles, so I'd assumed she was a permanent resident, too.

"Ah, no, she just rides here as much as she can," Bree said, "but with the new horses coming it would be better for her to live here. She's trying to work it out with her parents."

She turned away before I could ask anything more, so I tucked the information away to think about later.

That night, I couldn't fall asleep for the longest time. There was no whisper of my sister's soft breathing or the other sounds of an overly crowded apartment settling to sleep. The house was so silent around me that it felt like the darkness was pressing in on all sides.

You are safe, I reminded myself, *this is a good place.*

Still, the lonely tears came, pooling in my eyes no matter how many times I wiped them away.

You're surrounded by horses. You're going to learn how to ride properly. This is a good thing for you. And it's a good thing for the family. You can do this.

I thought of the horses out in the barn, probably finished most of their hay by now and dozing, taking turns sleeping in the way that horses do.

They have their herd around them, I thought wistfully. If it hadn't been freezing outside, I think I would have gotten dressed again and crept down to the barn to curl up in the hay and fell asleep with them. At least that way I wouldn't have felt so alone.

I closed my eyes with a sigh, willing it to be morning and for this lonely night to be over.

Suddenly, the phone on my desk began to shudder and vibrate. I'd only gotten it a couple of days before so I didn't even recognize the ring tone. I barely knew how to work it yet. I was up and lunging for it before I'd even opened my eyes.

I'd left a voicemail for my mom earlier to say that I'd arrived safely, but nobody had called me back.

The clock on my phone said eleven as I swiped eagerly to take the phone call.

"Hey, Mom," I whispered, my heart thudding with happiness that she'd remembered me.

"Adie!" It wasn't mom's voice, it was Flora.

"Hey, sweet pea," I said, delighted to hear her voice. "What are you doing up so late?"

"I can't sleep. I miss you. I'm mad that you're not here. Grady's mad, too.

"I know, I'm sorry, kiddo. I miss you, too. Where are you?"

"Out the window. Mom's asleep but I borrowed her phone."

"You're on the fire escape by yourself?"

"No, Grady's here, too. He's sad. We have snacks and blankets. We want to hear about the horses. Do any of them look like Teddy?"

"They're beautiful," I said truthfully, "and they're a lot bigger than Teddy. But why is Grady sad?"

There was a mumble of voices while the two of them had an argument.

"He said never mind, he's fine. He's writing a song and doesn't want me to bother him. I made up a song, too. I can sing it to you if you like. It's about horses."

"That would be amazing, Flora. I'd love to hear it."

"Okay, here it goes."

And she put the phone down with a clunk and started into a soothing lullaby in her clear, beautiful voice about horses and the country.

"That was beautiful," I told her honestly, stifling a yawn. "But it's really late and I think we all need to get to sleep. Are you going inside now?"

"Grady says yes. Goodnight, Adie. We'll call you tomorrow. Say hi to the horses for me."

And before I could ask to say goodnight to Grady too, she'd hung up.

I closed my eyes with a smile, my loneliness completely gone. Flora's little melody still swirled around me and I fell asleep with the echo of music in my ears.

CHAPTER 11

BREE

*W*hen the Narnia-like freeze that had held the world in a strangle-hold since December finally broke up, it did it with a sudden clash of cymbals finale. One final miserable day of freezing, and then winter was over. Just like that.

I woke up one morning, a week after Adie arrived, to find that the icy landscape outside had been replaced by a grey, dripping, melting world overnight and everything was steadily turning to mush.

The temperature shot up and I could finally ditch my double-layered scarf and thick toque. Birds appeared everywhere, whirling around from tree to tree and screaming loudly at one another excitedly.

The melting came with its own challenges, but I hardly cared. Spring was finally coming and that was all that mattered.

The path to the manure pile went from a slick hard trail of ice to a sloppy, wet track full of ruts and pools of water. The wheel-barrow routinely got stuck about five times every trip and you had to heave it back and forth to get it moving again.

My nose dripped and my lungs were working overtime, but I was still crazily happy not to be freezing anymore. With any luck, the last of winter was behind us and hopefully I'd never have to experience another cold snap like that again.

"We'll give the ring a week or so to thaw and let the water drain away," Julie said, "and then we should try and rake it. I'll bet you're dying to ride again."

"I am. I want to ride Nipper, and I really want to start working with Ace. I've been dreaming about starting him for a long time and I can hardly wait."

"I'm excited for you, too. There is nothing like working with your first project."

The horses' hooves churned the melting ground into a soupy mess near the pasture gate. Each night they came in with dark mud coating their legs right up to their arm pits. Their blankets became caked with thick layers of dirt and even their faces were splattered with mud.

They slipped and skidded on the slick ground and more than once, one of the senior horses had come in from the pasture limping.

"This is not good," Julie said as she carefully sponged the thick mud off Slate's legs one night. "Somebody is going to get hurt. And we can't expect the new horses to stay sound if we turn them out in that. It's dangerous."

Lorne had grumbled for a few days about how he didn't believe in babying horses, but when Bear hobbled in one night, that was the last straw.

A few days later, a crew showed up with a huge machine to pound posts and rolls of fencing. In short order, a set of small paddocks were built on the far side of the barn. And then the machine trundled up the hill and repaired the fallen pasture behind the ring and the one further up beyond the house.

"It looks like the good old days," Julie said, beaming at Lorne.

And though he'd muttered about the cost, I caught him standing out behind the barn admiring the new paddocks more than once.

Day by day, I watched the snow in the ring melt. First, the edges thawed and shrank back, and then the mound over the mounting block disappeared. I took to hand-walking the horses in there for a few minutes when I brought them in out of the field, letting their hooves churn up the bits that were left.

I was so eager that I actually went in with a pitchfork and scooped up all the movable chunks of snow and wheelbarrowed them to the manure pile, dumping them with satisfaction.

"Now that's the work ethic I like to see," Lorne had said, laughing at me as he limped by. "You do know it will just thaw on its own eventually, right?"

"It's taking too long," I told him. And I worked all one sunny afternoon until I had a giant square cleared around the bottom of the ring.

There, now the sun can get to the sand and warm it up, I thought with satisfaction. And it turned out that I'd been right. By the next day the upper half of the ring was still snowy, but the lower half was beautifully soft. I was able to pull out the lawnmower from the shed, hook up the harrow, and make a few passes around the space I'd cleared.

"Nice work," Julie told me, looking at the cleared area with shining eyes. It was a big enough circle for lunging and doing basic schooling. It was a start anyway. "You should change into breeches and we'll go get Ace out."

"Seriously?" I said, practically jumping up and down in excitement. "We can work with him today? I can ride him?"

"Well, let's take him out and lunge him and see what happens.

We don't know where he left off in his training before he was injured. But you have to be rewarded somehow for all that hard work and there's no time like the present, is there?"

"No. There definitely is not." I practically ran up to the house and threw on breeches and filled my coat pockets with bits of cut-up carrots from the kitchen. This was all so sudden that I could hardly believe it was happening.

Ace, Ace, I get to ride Ace. The words ran through my head in a happy chant.

By the time I got back to the barn, Julie had already brought Ace in from the pasture and had him cross-tied in the aisle. She worked a curry-comb in circles through his thick winter coat.

"He's starting to shed," she said, shaking the brush so that little tufts of hair drifted to the ground. "That's a good sign that spring is really here."

I grabbed another brush and set to work on his other side, working carefully through his plush coat so that there were absolutely no traces of dirt or loose hair that would get caught under his tack. I wanted him to be as comfortable as possible.

Ace stood with his eyes half-closed and his lower lip drooping as he enjoyed his massage. He barely looked up when I set the new blue saddle pad I'd bought him on his back, and then set the saddle carefully on top of that. He didn't care about the girth being done up and he gently opened his mouth to accept the bit and stood quietly while I adjusted his bridle.

"Well, he is just a superstar, isn't he?" Julie said, scratching under his mane and giving him a pat. "Someone took the time to start him properly in the past. Let's see what else he knows."

He perked up a little when we stepped out into the warm spring air and headed toward the ring. We'd been in there before for hand-walking of course, but he could sense that this time was somehow different. He pricked his ears and there was almost a spring in his step.

Julie followed us, carrying a coiled lunge line and whip.

"We'll work with him on the lunge-line first," Julie said. "He was probably lunged in the past as part of his training, but you never know. Some trainers skip that part."

She ran the lunge-line through the ring in Ace's bit, over his head and clipped it to the bit-ring on the other side. Then she fixed his reins to the saddle so they wouldn't dangle and trip him.

"You lead him from the outside for now, Bree. Let's just see if he knows any voice-commands first. Ready? Walk-on, Ace." She pointed the lunge-whip at his hip.

Ace hesitated for a moment, and then his ears swiveled toward her and he took a few tentative steps forward.

"Good boy, walk-on." I stayed beside him as he strode along and then stopped with him when Julie called out for us to halt. We did that a few more times before Julie nodded in satisfaction.

"He looks like he's done this before, Bree. You can go sit on the mounting block and we'll ask him to move out a little."

"Good boy," I whispered to him, slipping a piece of carrot between his teeth before I went over to my seat on the mounting block.

"Walk-on," Julie called again, narrowly preventing Ace from trying to follow me. She had him circle a few more times. "Okay, ter-rottt."

Ace opened his eyes wide in surprise and, after a moment's hesitation, he bounced up into an ungainly trot, his legs flailing a little in all directions.

"Eaasssy," Julie said, her voice rising and falling in a soothing tone. Ace relaxed right away, dropping his head and snorting a few times as he fell into a slow, shuffling trot.

"Good boy, Ace," I called as he slowly passed by me. It was so exciting to see him in action for the first time. I'd seen him running in the pasture before of course, but this was different.

"Okay, can-ter," Julie called, and he broke into a smooth, slow canter that was almost the same speed as his trot. He looked a bit like a rocking-horse.

Julie had him do a few more circles and then she brought him back down to a walk and gave him a hearty pat. She fed him a chunk of carrot and let him catch his breath. Then she did the same thing all over again in the other direction.

"You can see this is his harder side," she said, as she stopped him from turning in and trying to change direction for the third time.

"Is he sore?" I asked worriedly.

"I don't think so. Maybe just stiff. And maybe he was worked more in the other direction and this feels strange and unfamiliar. We'll figure it out as we go along. Even though he doesn't like it, it's still important to work him equally on both sides. We'll just keep in mind that this way is harder for him."

Ace finally resigned himself to moving forward in that direction and hopped into a trot when he was asked and then into a shambling canter.

It was interesting to see how differently he handled his body going a different direction. The other way, he'd looked like he was more balanced and rhythmical, but this way his head stuck up in the air and he poked his nose awkwardly to the outside.

After a few circuits, Julie brought him down to a walk again and then lavished praise all over him.

"That was excellent for his first session," she said, beaming with pride at him. "He could not have handled that better. He's not exactly an extravagant mover, but he was steady and calm the whole time. He's out of condition and unbalanced, but he has a great head on his shoulders. You picked a good one."

"That was so amazing, buddy," I told him, scratching the itchy spot he liked under his mane. He tilted his head and closed his eyes, wriggling his lip a little in the air.

"You ready to get on?" Julie said, smiling at me and raising an eyebrow in challenge.

"Really?" I practically squealed. "It's not too much for him for his first day back in work?"

"I don't think so. He seems pretty relaxed, and we'll just take it slow and see what he thinks about someone on his back. I have a feeling he won't mind at all. Someone did a great job starting him off on the right foot. He's a good boy."

"He is," I agreed. "Okay, let's do this."

I led Ace to the mounting block with my heart hammering in my chest. Not because I was scared at all, but because this was the moment I'd waited for since the first time I saw him at that sale barn.

This is happening, I thought gleefully, *another thing to check off my wish-list.*

"Right, so I'll hold his reins. You just start by getting up on the mounting block beside him. Pet him and play with the saddle, take your foot in and out of the stirrups a few times. We'll treat him like a baby horse for now. We're going to go slow and watch all his reactions to see if he has any gaps in his education. We want to stay in his comfort zone today."

I climbed up and stood next to Ace for a few seconds, patting him and moving the stirrups around and leaning over the saddle with half my weight still on the mounting block.

Ace didn't care. He swiveled his ears back a few times, but other than that he stood stalk-still, with his head hanging and his eyes half-closed. If anything, he looked bored.

"All right, I don't think he's going to care about any of this," Julie said, laughing. "Climb aboard, kiddo."

Those were the words I'd been waiting for. I gathered Ace's reins in one hand and then climbed carefully into the saddle.

I'm on him, I'm really on him. For a second, happy tears stung my eyes before I brushed them impatiently away.

"Good boy," I told him, nosing my other foot into the stirrup and settling myself until I felt secure in the saddle. I leaned down to pet his neck, marveling at how much smaller than Nipper he felt even though he was actually about the same height. He just had a much slighter build, and his neck was set on in a different way.

"Ready to go for a walk?" Julie asked, grinning up at me.

"Definitely. Let's go."

Julie kept one hand on Ace's reins at first while we moved him around the outside of the square, but it was hardly necessary. He moved at a snail's pace, even slower than he had on the lunge-line. As if he were out for a leisurely stroll and had all the time in the world. It was completely different from Nipper's animated, forward march.

"Well, he certainly isn't in a hurry, is he?" Julie said, laughing and stepping back from us. "This is his harder side. Turn him in the other direction and see if he moves off better that way."

I turned Ace the other way and was pleased to feel that there was a marginal increase in his speed. In fact, the longer we walked the better it began to feel.

"Good, that's better. It's going to take time for him to gain some muscle and conditioning. He hasn't carried a rider for a while and he's really still growing. He might go through a few awkward phases before he fills out properly. We're not going to fuss at him for more impulsion at this point."

"You're such a good boy," I told him, reaching down to run my fingers through his silky mane.

"Are you ready to try a trot this direction?" Julie asked. "I can hook him back on the lunge-line, if you like."

"No, I think it's okay," I said, although I was suddenly a little nervous. I was just breaking records all over today. My first walk and my first trot on my own project horse.

I shortened my reins a fraction and gently asked Ace to trot. There was zero response. I asked him again, this time not just with my seat but with a little leg, too. An ear flicked back, and he walked a little faster.

"Ask again, more firmly," Julie said, laughing. "I don't think he believes you. Don't be afraid to use your voice, too."

"Ter-rott" I said, just like Julie had when she'd lunged him. And then I gave him a harder nudge with the inside of my ankle. A nudge like that would have sent Nipper bolting off across the ring, but with Ace it just led to him breaking into a slow trot.

"Good start," Julie said, going over to pick up the lunge whip at the mounting block. "Trot on, sir" she added, stepping behind Ace a little and lifting the lunge whip ever so slightly. Ace flicked an ear toward her and suddenly his trot felt less like wading through molasses and more like he was using his hind end to propel himself along.

"That's better," I said, breathing out a sigh of relief. I rose and fell easily with his rhythm now and it was effortless.

I crossed the ring and asked him to change directions, but as soon as we were going the other way, he slowed to that sticky trot again and stuck his nose up in the air. I glanced over at Julie, not sure what to do.

"That's fine, just ask him to go forward again. He's just not balanced, and he has no idea what sort of trot we're asking for. It's up to us to show him clearly what we want."

"Ter-ot," I said firmly again, closing my legs against his side. He moved forward at fractionally more speed and Julie laughed.

"Good job, Bree. Don't fuss with him too much. We'll figure him out as we go along. That's probably enough for him for his first day. You can ask him to walk."

He'd dropped down instantly to a walk as soon as Julie said the word, lowering his head and letting out a hearty snort as if I've been galloping him for hours. We'd probably been in the ring a total of a half hour.

"Lots of short, positive sessions are the best thing for him," Julie said, coming over to pat Ace on the neck. "Do you remember how sore you were when you first started out?"

"Oh, right," I said, remembering how much my out-of-conditioned muscles had ached even after my first few walking trail rides on Bear. I'd hobbled around for weeks before I'd finally adapted to my new routine.

"Exactly. We want him to always feel good about his learning sessions. He should look forward to them and he won't do that if we overwork him before he's ready. Good job today out there. You guys looked good together. Why don't you ride him back to the barn?"

She opened the gate for me, and I passed by her, grinning from ear to ear. Even though he'd felt a bit awkward and unbalanced, Ace had behaved like a gentleman and I knew that the time when we would be exploring the trails together was coming soon.

"You're such a good boy," I told him when we reached the front door of the barn. I swung down and hit the slushy ground with a plop. Icy water sprayed up in all directions, spattering my breeches and Ace's legs and belly.

He lifted his head and gave me a bewildered look.

Nope, not even getting soaked with ice water can destroy my good mood, I thought, flicking the dirty slush from my legs and from Ace's coat. *Your days are numbered, winter.*

Adie was in the barn grooming Bear, carefully running a comb through his mane with a dreamy, far-off expression on her face. She was tapping the fingers of her free hand rhythmically against her hip and she didn't look up as Ace and I clopped into the aisle. Not until I'd led him to the cross-ties next to her.

"Oh, sorry, I didn't see you," she said shaking her head like she was coming out of a trance.

"No problem, Bear looks like he's enjoying himself."

"Oh, yes." She looked at Bear as if she were surprised to see him there in front of her too, and gave him a hesitant pat. "Sorry, my mind is all over the place. I was thinking about this song my little sister is working on. I can't get the melody out of my head for some reason."

"You don't have to apologize, Adie," I said, slipping off Ace's bridle and substituting it for his halter. "You can do whatever you like with your free time."

"Right, I know. I'm actually not used to having free time," she said wistfully. "I don't know what to do with myself. Julie set me to work brushing the horses."

"Hey, I have to run into town this afternoon to get some bloodwork done. It's no big deal. It should be a really quick appointment, but you could come along if you like, and I could show you the town or we could go to the beach. Sometimes there are whales."

"Ooh, the beach would be nice. I haven't been to the ocean in ages. You really don't mind if I tag along? I wouldn't be in the way?"

Adie's face had lit up when I'd asked her to come along, and I felt a stab of guilt. Maybe I hadn't been paying much attention to her this week. I was used to being on my own, so it didn't bother me most of the time. It hadn't occurred to me that she might be lonely and missing her family.

"Of course not. I'd love some company. I hate needles so it would be nice to have something fun to do afterward."

And that afternoon, even though I assured her that she didn't need to come inside and that she was free to wait in the car, Adie stood right beside me at the lab while a hurried nurse stabbed me harder than necessary and took vial after vial of my blood.

Adie somehow seemed to know how I felt about this place, and about medical procedures in general, because she kept me talking the whole time while the nurse silently worked. Asking questions about Ace and the farm and keeping me occupied so I didn't dwell on how scared I was to be there.

"Your doctor will call you when the results come in. Have a

good day," the nurse said brusquely, slapping a band-aid over the tiny, oozing hole in my arm.

"Come on," Adie said, grabbing my other hand, "let's get out of here."

We were out the door before I knew it and headed for the beach. I didn't have time to think about all the underlying feelings of fear and despair that that short appointment had brought up. The salty wind buffeted my hair around my face and the bark of sealions filled the air.

"Ooh, look at the ocean. And there's a donut shop," Adie called back to me. Her hair flew wildly in all directions. "Come on, let's get some dessert. My treat today."

Her smile was contagious, and I found myself following after her, squinting my eyes against the reflection of the sun off the sea. I realized then that Adie wasn't just someone for me to babysit. If I let her, she could be a real friend.

That day at the ocean somehow became a turning point in my life. It was like, after surviving that dreary, depressing winter, all the good, exciting things started to happen at once.

Ace's first ride, the amazing weather, the new fencing, me finally going to get that bloodwork done so I could stop worrying about nothing. My new friendship with Adie. And we got the call from the shipper that the racehorses were on their way and would be arriving the coming weekend. Things just started looking better and better.

But most astonishing of all was when, on Friday afternoon, Nicholas's little green Volkswagen unexpectedly chugged its way up the driveway.

I thought I had prepared myself for that moment. But no matter how hard I'd steeled my heart not to care, it still gave a jolt of joy when I caught sight of his car.

I happened to be pushing a wheelbarrow down the barn aisle

when the car passed by and I quickly jumped back and hid in the shadows, willing him not to stop. Not to come see me until I'd had a chance to get control of my wildly spinning emotions.

You've been to the brink of death, surely you can handle this, I told myself firmly.

I took a deep breath and resolutely picked up the handles of the wheelbarrow again, pushing it outside to the manure pile. I had lots of chores to get done.

I kept my breathing and my heartbeat steady when, not ten minutes later, the car came back down the hill toward the road.

Oh, he must be leaving, I told myself calmly, *that's nice. He must have just stopped by to pick up some things and say hi to Julie.*

I turned back to the barn, willing myself not to look behind me. I had hours of work left to do and the barn wouldn't clean itself.

Tires crunched up behind me and the rumbling engine died abruptly. I felt my breath catch in my throat, but I stiffened my spine and forced myself to turn around with a polite smile on my face.

"Bree." Nicholas jumped out of the car and moved toward me, beaming happily. His dark hair was tousled and there were dark circles under his eyes like he'd just gotten out of bed.

Before I had the chance to step away, he'd closed the distance between us and wrapped me in a tight hug.

"I've missed you," he said into my hair and, despite my intentions, I leaned into the warmth of him, closing my eyes. "I finally got a chance to come home for the weekend. Mom told me that the new horses are coming. I couldn't miss that."

When he finally let go, I had to force myself to step backward.

"Oh, hey," I said as casually as I could, fighting hard to keep the tremor out of my voice. "Good to see you."

"Yeah, I feel like I've been gone forever. School has been a killer this year. Here, let me take that. I'll help you finish the barn while we catch up."

"You don't have to do that," I said stiffly, clinging to the handles for a second until he deftly wrestled them away from me.

"I know. But it will be easier to talk this way. I'm hardly going to stand there watching while you do all the work. I feel like I haven't seen you in ages."

"Three weeks," I said and immediately wished I hadn't.

"I know. Sorry about that. I should have called or texted. But there is always something happening there. I feel like I'm barely keeping my head above water. You understand what it's like. Your dad is a teacher."

He went off down the aisle whistling under his breath, completely oblivious to the fact that I was churning in an emotional whirlwind.

I took a deep breath and pulled myself together with difficulty. I was stronger than this. I was perfectly capable of having an adult friendship with my boss's son. People squashed down their inappropriate feelings all the time. I could, too.

He'll stay for the weekend and then disappear back to school again. Surely, I can survive one weekend.

But as Nicholas and I worked side by side we fell into those old, easy patterns of just *being* with each other that we'd had before.

It was just so simple to be myself around him. Way too easy, actually. It was tough to keep my guard up and protect my tender feelings. I had the feeling that *someone* was going to get hurt and that someone was probably me.

He chatted away about his life at school, his friends, and his workload. Filling me in on everything I'd missed since his last visit weeks ago. Despite the tired droop to his shoulders and the circles under his eyes from too many late nights studying, he looked happy, and I knew university life suited him perfectly. It was where he belonged.

I felt a pang of regret that I wasn't there with him, sharing all those adventures and learning about new things. I'd actually enjoyed going to school in the short time I'd been in University. Before my life had been cut short by nearly dying.

That part of my life is all behind me, though, I told myself, *I can't go backwards and undo it. This is my life now and I'm lucky to have it. And I love it here. I'd never give up the farm. Nicholas and I just have separate lives and are going in different directions. The sooner I realize that, the better.*

CHAPTER 12

ADIE

*T*he dishes were done, and I'd just finished cleaning the kitchen when Julie appeared beside me, a grin on her face.

"Don't you think it's time we get you up on a horse?" she asked. "It's time to start your education."

"Really?" I practically squealed. I had been working hard to fit in on the farm and pull my weight with chores. I'd been too busy to even really think about riding. But now that the opportunity was in front of me, I felt a flash of excitement.

"Absolutely. I have an old pair of breeches that I think might fit you. Luckily, I never get rid of anything because the last time they fit me I was probably twelve."

So, in the late afternoon, I found myself dressed in my first pair of breeches ever and wearing a set of rubber boots and Julie was dusting off an old helmet and fitting it to my head.

With the abrupt change in the weather, the horses had begun to shed in earnest. Bear's two-inch-thick coat came out in layers as I carefully ran the metal shedding comb over his bony sides. He closed his eyes and leaned into me, clearly enjoying the spa treatment, his lower lip drooping.

"You're such a good boy," I told him. He was my favourite of the senior horses, my favourite of all the horses there actually, even though he was old and not fancy at all. He reminded me a lot of Teddy, who had been like a kindly older brother to all of us kids.

Teddy hadn't been the type of naughty pony that some people thought about when they heard the word *pony*. He had pretty much been a saint. If one of us fell off, he'd stop and wait for them to get back on. He never bit or kicked or any of those things. And he was always up for an adventure. We rode him everywhere. We even took him to swim in the pond and would pack up picnic lunches and ride with him to the river, with as many of us piled on his broad back as possible.

He'd had an easy, rocking horse canter, and his back always felt like sitting on a comfortable couch.

Bear had the same way of looking at a person that Teddy did. His expression was wise and kind. Like an elderly teacher.

Julie hung around cleaning a bridle she'd taken apart until I was done grooming and then she brought out a shiny, black saddle and an armful of saddle pads.

"Do you remember how everything goes on?" she asked. Which was kind of the moment I'd been dreading because as much fun as I'd had cantering Teddy all over the countryside, we'd hardly ever bothered to use a saddle. The few times we had it had been an old western saddle. I actually knew nothing about English tack at all.

"Um," I said, clearing my throat. "I rode Western? And it's been a long time."

"No problem. I'll show you this time and then you'll know how to do it for next time. Here, hold the saddle for a second and I'll put his pads on."

She handed me the soft leather saddle, which was surprisingly heavy and proceeded to place the larger red pad on Bear's back, and then set the smaller fluffy white pad overtop of it.

"He needs a bit of extra cushioning," Julie said, smiling and taking the saddle from me.

She placed the saddle on top of the white pad and then proceeded to shimmy it around a little and slide it backward away from his withers.

"You need to find the perfect spot for it to sit," Julie said. "Not too far forward, not too far back. You want his shoulders to be able to move freely and not get pinched by the saddle when he's moving."

I watched carefully while she placed it and did up the girth so I could do it myself the next time.

"Are you okay doing the bridle on your own?"

"Sure," I said, although truly, we'd often just used a halter and lead rope when we rode Teddy. Or even just a rope around his neck. Still, I knew how a bit worked. Even though the English bridle had double the amount of leather pieces as my old western headstall, I managed to put it on and adjust it without too much fuss.

"Let's just make sure his noseband and throatlatch aren't too tight," Julie said, leaning forward to slide a couple of buckles further down the leather. "We want this old man to be comfortable. Right, now let's get you to the ring."

The next forty-five minutes were very educational. I'd had no idea that riding could be so complicated. With Teddy we had just hopped on and went on adventures. I had never given much thought as to how I sat or held the reins or what my legs were doing. I wasn't sure why everything had to be so complicated. No wonder riders in the horse magazines always had such tense expressions on their faces. This was hard work. And also a little painful.

I am here to try new things and have new experiences, I told myself firmly when my mind wandered from Julie's instructions, *pay attention.*

Despite all the endless little fiddly details, I had fun riding Bear. He was slow and steady, and he put up with me trying to figure out all the instructions Julie was firing at me. We even did a shambling trot that had me giggling the whole time as I tried to rise up and down in the saddle.

I couldn't wait to tell Flora and Grady about my first ride. Their schedule was so messed up that I hadn't been able to talk to them in almost a week. By my estimate, their tour bus should have been nearing the east coast by then. In another few days, they would be crossing the border and dipping down into the states.

"You're getting it," Julie said, smiling at me encouragingly. "Of course, Bear is a senior, so we can't ask him to do too much. But you can refine your position on him and get your riding muscles back in shape."

"Do you think we could maybe do a trail ride some day?" I asked, already longing to be out of the ring and exploring the neighbourhood. I envied Chloe and Bree who could just canter off on their own at any time.

"Of course you can. But Bear won't be up for as much as the other horses. You can walk him around the short loop that crosses the river, though. We'll get Bree to show you next time she goes out."

"That would be great, thanks," I said, leaning down and scratching Bear's neck appreciatively.

"Once Bree has Ace going a little better, we can have you take some lessons on Nipper. He's nice and forward."

"Ah, sure," I said, feeling an uncomfortable shiver going down my spine. *Or I could just keep riding Bear.* I didn't actually like Nipper. He was pushy and he didn't seem kind like Bear did.

But the way Julie was looking at me, I wondered if I had any say in the matter at all.

I was still glowing with happiness by the time dinner came around and it took me a while to realize that Bree wasn't quite her normal, talkative self.

Which was weird because I would have thought that she would have been thrilled that Julie's son Nicholas was home for the weekend. I'd gotten the impression that they were a couple. Or at least were interested in each other.

I wasn't sure what her issue was because anyone with half a brain could see him shooting sideways anxious looks at her. He clearly adored her. But instead of joining in on the conversation she kept this polite smile fixed determinedly on her face like she'd painted it there and stared down at her plate. She wasn't even eating. She just pushed her food around with her fork.

Julie and Lorne did all the talking. Alternating between asking Nicholas all about school and his life at the dorm and making plans for the racehorses.

Chloe had gotten permission from her overbearing mother to stay over for the weekend, but she seemed oblivious to the odd way Bree was acting. She just concentrated on shoveling Julie's homemade pot roast and biscuits into her mouth as fast as she could. You'd think she never got fed at home or something.

Later that night, I sat tucked in bed reading a book and waiting for someone to call me. Mom had texted me earlier to say that they were on their way to a gig, but I hadn't heard anything since.

They have a busy schedule, I told myself, *and they're travelling and seeing new things. I can't expect them to think of me all the time.*

Something tapped on the roof outside my window, probably a branch of the big pine that grew near the backside of the house. The tree was so tall and wide that it was practically all trunk. It didn't have a single sideways branch until it reached the roof where a triangle of greenery sat on the top of it like a crown.

Julie had told me that she'd meant to have it cut down years ago since it was most likely destined to fall on the house once it got old and started to rot. But somehow, every year she forgot.

The branch made a rhythmic tapping sound and I looked down to see that I'd automatically started tapping my fingers against my leg to the imaginary beat.

I shook my head and laughed. I'd worked hard trying to adapt to my new life and push music completely away. But it was easier said than done.

There wasn't any way to shut my ears off completely. Not when the feed tubs hitting the floor one after another landed in accidental rhythm. Not when the horses' hooves clopping down the aisle were a natural percussion. Not when the wind blew through the eaves of the old farmhouse at night making crooning, wailing sounds like far off voices. A teaspoon ringing against the edge of a cup, the way Julie tapped her foot so restlessly against the side of her chair whenever she was thinking hard. Even the roar of the old vacuum, eggs frying in a pan, or the horses crunching their hay sounded like music to me.

It was like my brain was hardwired to hear patterns and melodies and rhythms everywhere.

And it wasn't just the sounds, it was words, too. No matter how hard I tried to keep myself busy, I kept getting these ideas for songs flowing into my head against my will. I honestly had to force myself from writing them down.

So many times, I would start to ask Julie or someone for some paper and a pen. And each time I would turn away and stop myself from asking at the last minute.

It's like a drug, I had told myself firmly, *you just have to go cold turkey and cut it off. It will go away eventually.*

But instead of going away, it just kept getting stronger and stronger. It wasn't so bad in the daytime when I could keep myself busy. But at night in my bed when the loneliness crept in, I found myself craving some creative outlet.

"Fine," I said, glancing one more time at my phone to make sure I hadn't missed a text or a call. I hadn't.

Somebody was watching television in the living room, but I didn't need to go as far as that. I trotted down the stairs and went into the little library, sure I had seen a pad of paper and a pen on the cluttered desk.

And the second my pen touched the page, it was like all these words just flowed out of me like a waterfall. I didn't even keep track of what I was writing. I just wrote and wrote until I was limp with effort, filling page after page with thoughts, images, and bits of music.

"There," I said finally, tossing the book carelessly off the bed and onto the floor. I crawled back under the covers with a happy sigh of relief. "I'm glad that's over with."

I jolted back upright when my phone began to vibrate on the desk.

I quickly grabbed it and flopped down on my bed again, hitting the answer button with a flourish.

"Hello?"

"Adie, it's me!" Flora's loud whisper crackled through the phone.

"Hey, pumpkin, how are you? What city are you in?"

"Good and I don't know. We're camped in a big parking lot, though. The twins aren't sharing their games with me. Ivy said I was too young to play with them."

"Uh oh, that's not very nice. Did you tell Mariam or Micah?"

"I can't. They're out singing but we couldn't go. It's in a bar and we're too young."

"In a bar?" I said, crinkling my forehead. Part of our brand had always been to only play at family-friendly events. It was something we'd all agreed on in the beginning. "So, who is there looking after you?"

"Grady. But he's outside playing his guitar. He's mad at Phil."

"Not surprising. What did Phil do this time?"

"I'm not supposed to tell."

"Oh, really?" I said, suspiciously. "Who told you not to tell?"

"Grady. He said mom and dad would be mad if they found out."

"Well, how about you tell me instead," I said, struggling to keep my voice calm.

"Okay, but you can't get mad. Phil hit Grady really hard. He has a big bruise on his back."

A sort of red haze crossed in front of my eyes and I felt my breath coming out in a series of short gasps.

"He did *what?*"

"Promise you won't tell. Grady doesn't want anyone to know. He said he wants to handle it on his own. Can I sing you the song I'm working on now? The twins don't want to hear it."

"Um, sure, of course," I said, my mind whirling around feverishly. "But, Flora, I want you to get mom to call me as soon as she gets back, okay. I don't care what time it is. I need to talk to her."

"Yep, okay. So here's my song."

Her voice rose and fell in the same song about the horse she'd been working on for weeks. But it didn't sound so sweet and light anymore. There was a new edge of anxious tension to her voice that wound through the music.

What on earth had happened to my family in the short time I'd been away? It sounded like everything was falling apart.

CHAPTER 13

BREE

*A*ll my complicated thoughts about Nicholas were completely pushed aside the next day when the huge trailer finally chugged up the driveway pulling our five new horses.

I could hardly believe it was finally happening.

"There they are," Lorne said, rubbing his hands together gleefully. His eyes were bright with excitement, and I reached out and hugged him impulsively. I knew exactly how much this meant to him. To be able to see Gretta's vision come to life.

"Come on, let them all be talented eventing prospects," Chloe joked, crossing her fingers and grinning over at Lorne.

"I'd settle for sound and sane," Julie added.

I tightened my fingers on my phone, poised and ready to take millions of photos for our blog. Each horse was going to get their own profile and I'd write a series of articles tracking everyone's progress.

Nicholas shifted beside me, his arm touching mine and I had

to force myself to stay still. Half of me wanted to lean into him and the other half of me wanted to get as far away as I could. Things were extremely complicated inside my head. It was much easier to ignore him and focus on the horses instead.

We'd turned Ace, Dragon, and most of the seniors out on pasture so that the new arrivals wouldn't be too overwhelmed entering into a barn full of horses. But we'd decided to leave Bear and Nipper inside. Hopefully, they'd be a sort of calming influence on the young horses.

From what we knew, the oldest horse on that trailer was five years old and the others ranged between two and four years old. They were all more than twenty-five years younger than Bear.

The trailer rolled to a stop in front of the barn, and we could hear hooves thudding on the rubber-lined floor inside. Someone neighed and from the back near the door came the sound of something banging against the metal walls.

The shipper opened his door and leapt down, leather boots splashing onto the wet ground. The sun was out but it had rained the night before, clearing the last of the snow away, and the ground was sloppy. He was middle-aged with a blue hat pulled down tightly over his grey hair.

"Heck of a crew you have here," he said tiredly, not cracking a smile. He looked tired and stiff from his long hours spent on the road.

"Oh?" Lorne said, his excited expression falling away a little. "Did they give you trouble?"

"No, they seem to be decent enough horses. We had a little difficulty at the border, and they handled it well."

"What kind of trouble?" Julie asked.

"You know, the usual. The border guards were just doing their job. Every so often, they want to search the trailers for drugs and contraband. They made me unload every single horse on the tarmac so they could go over the trailer from head to tail. They even brought in a sniffer dog to check it out."

"Wow, really? That seems excessive," Lorne said.

"I guess they'd had a tip about someone with a trailer of some sort trying to smuggle drugs into the country. I was just at the right place at the wrong time. Anyway, it wasn't that much of a big deal. I tied most of the horses up and held onto the young one and it was all over in twenty minutes. It could have gone badly though, if these guys hadn't been so level-headed."

"Well, they probably saw a lot at the track," Julie said, "they get exposed to so much that it takes a lot to shake them."

"Yeah, that's for sure. Anyway, where would you like me to put them?"

"We can unload them right here. Their stalls are ready and waiting."

I jumped up and down in excitement when the shipper unclipped the lock on the back of the trailer, opened the double doors, and then pushed the button that slowly let down the ramp.

"This is it," Nicholas said beside me, and I couldn't help but meet his smile.

He had a clipboard in his hand, and it was his job to check off the horses and match their names to their descriptions. All we had was their registered names, colours, and basic racing statistics. And we knew which were mares and geldings. But Eddie hadn't sent us photos or given us any other sort of useful information. He probably hadn't even met all of these horses himself in person before.

"All right, first one off," Julie said and stepped forward to receive a big bay gelding who held his head way up in the air. He was looking around with his eyes bulging and a bewildered, anxious expression on his face. He had a set of banana-shaped oversized ears that were swiveling wildly in all directions as he tried to take in his new surroundings.

He jerked his head up when Julie took the lead rope but then he clattered down off the ramp and stood there, huddling close beside her, his nose touching her shoulder.

I raised my camera and got a dozen shots of him standing there, looking like he was posing.

Lorne peered down impatiently at the clipboard in Nicholas's hands.

"Which one is it?" he asked, squinting. He couldn't really see well enough to read anymore.

"Um," Nicholas said, "there's only one bay listed. A gelding, 16.3 hands high and five years old. Retired sound. This must be Run Rabbit Run."

Lorne grinned and nodded. "Well, he's a fine-looking fellow. Seems sensible enough. You okay taking him inside, Chloe? Just put him in any of the stalls we got ready. We'll sort them out later."

"Yep, sure. No problem." Chloe took the lead rope from Julie, gave the gelding a reassuring pat on the shoulder, and led him away. The horse danced a few anxious steps and then settled down to follow her obediently.

"Maybe throw a blanket on him, too," Julie called after her. "This is a long way temperature-wise from California."

The next one the shipper brought out was a small, shiny black filly with a white blaze on her delicate face, wide eyes, and a worried expression. Her neck was slick with sweat and she trembled as she picked her way to the bottom of the ramp.

"Aww, this one is a love," Julie said, stroking the mare's neck gently. "She's just a baby."

"This must be FollowTheMoney; filly, 15.2, two years old. Trained at the track but never raced. No injuries."

"Were you just not fast enough, girl? Or was it all too overwhelming?" Julie asked her soothingly. "Here, Chloe," she said as Chloe appeared back at the trailer again. Let's put this one as far away from Dragon's stall as we can."

The little mare scooted close to Chloe as soon as her lead rope was handed over, scrambling to press as close as possible to her new human attendant without getting left behind. She looked terrified. I hoped that I'd managed to get some decent shots of her.

"This one is as laid-back as they come," the shipper said, leading out a rangy chestnut gelding with impossibly long legs and a crooked blaze. The horse sauntered off the trailer and looked around boldly like he already owned the place.

"Wow, he's beautiful," Adie said breathlessly. "He's huge."

"Well now, that must be TizTimeForTea," Lorne said, pulling the clipboard away from Nicholas and raising it up close to his face so he could read, "chestnut gelding, four years old, 16.2, retired sound. He looks like a nice one. That might make a good project for Jeremy."

"Don't say that to Chloe," Julie warned. "She's going to want him."

"Chloe has Dragon," Lorne said, waving a gnarled hand dismissively in the air. "We'll have to give Jeremy something decent too, since he's coming so far. It's only fair."

"Oh, wow," Chloe said, catching sight of the gelding as she came back from the barn. "Now this is what I'm talking about. He looks amazing. I can't wait to see what he's like to ride."

"Right, well, there's a few more to unload," Lorne said hurriedly, "put him in the barn and we'll sort it all out later."

He was distracted by Julie's surprised burst of laughter.

"Oh my gosh, what is this supposed to be?" Julie said as a tall bay with a full white face and a pair of shocking blue eyes strode off the trailer. He had jagged white stockings that went up past his knees and there were huge irregular splashes of white across his neck and body.

"Ooh, I love him," Adie said, grabbing my arm in excitement. "Get lots of pictures of him, Bree."

"Umm …" Nicholas had taken his clipboard back and he looked down at the list and then back at the horse a few times. "Well, we only have two left and one is a grey. The other doesn't have anything listed for colour at all."

"You don't think that they sent us one of the pony horses by accident, do you?" Julie asked, meaning the horses that the outriders at the track rode. Sometimes they used thoroughbreds, but they also used all sorts of other breeds, including paints and quarter horses.

"I dunno. He looks pretty fancy under all that paint," Lorne said.

"Well, it says here that his name is My Chilly Boots, three years old, 16.2 hands, ten starts with some wins and some placings. Retired with small tendon bow on right front."

Lorne narrowed his eyes at the gelding who was busy trying to pull Julie toward the sparse, dead grass at the edge of the driveway. "Yep, there it is. Right front. Well, I suppose that's him, then. I'll call Eddie tonight just to confirm. I've heard of white body markings showing up in some thoroughbreds, but I've never seen it myself."

"Whoever he is, that is hardly a *small* tendon bow," Julie said, shaking her head. She knelt down and ran her hands lightly down the horse's front leg, wincing.

"Yikes, that is still fresh. I'm sure the long trailer ride didn't do him any good, either. He really shouldn't have come all that way. It's still hot and swollen, for heaven's sake."

I moved around so I could see from a better angle. The whole back side of his leg curved out backward with a bulgy area behind the cannon bone that made the whole lower leg look thicker and misshapen.

"Poor guy," I said. It looked awful.

"We're going to need to get a vet out right away. He should be on some pain control. He's most likely going to need a lot of time off, too."

Lorne sighed heavily. "Well, let's not worry about it too much right away. I guess we couldn't expect them all to be perfect. Put him away, Chloe. We'll sort him out later."

"Come on, handsome," Chloe said, leading the horse slowly

toward the barn. He limped with every step, but he didn't let that stop him from trying to drag Chloe off the driveway toward the grass, knocking into her with his big shoulder.

"Last one out," the shipper said, and Julie looked up just in time to take the lead rope of a big grey horse who clattered down the ramp, nearly tripping over his feet in his eagerness to reach the ground.

"Whoa, big guy," she said laughing, bringing him to a shuddering halt. He threw his head up and let out a bugling neigh, then dropped his nose and proceeded to itch his forehead on her arm as hard as he could.

"No, no, back up," she corrected, still laughing. "You are quite the character, aren't you?"

He snorted loudly and craned his head around, looking us all over one by one. He was a really funny shade of grey, almost a steel blue, with a salt and pepper mane and tail.

"Number Five is 15.3, a four-year-old gelding with three starts and zero wins. Retired sound. His name is"—Nicholas paused and snickered—"SugarDaddyNugget."

"Seriously?" I laughed. "What a name."

"Oh, I've heard some good ones in my time," Lorne said. "He looks like a solid boy, but he's built pretty downhill."

"What do you mean?" I asked, lowering my camera. The horse looked fine to me.

"Ah, well, see how his bum and hips are higher than the withers? His whole back is on a downward slope."

"Maybe a little," I said, squinting at the horse to try and see what Lorne meant.

"That puts a lot of weight on their forehand and it makes it harder to collect them. It's not a deal breaker, though. He's only four so he might have some more growing to do. It's possible he'll even out a tiny bit," Lorne said thoughtfully. "I guess we'll see what happens."

Julie led the grey inside herself and the rest of us followed along, leaving Lorne to thank the shipper and say goodbye. There wasn't anything that came with the horses, no blankets or extra feed or anything. Just their halters. We didn't even know what they were used to eating.

Although they were all owned by Eddie's group syndicate, they'd been staying at different barns and with different trainers. Some had been picked up by the shipper straight off the track and some had been on the trainer's farms already starting their transition from track life to civilian life. Most of these horses had probably never even met each other before being loaded up for their long trip to Canada.

By the time we got inside, Chloe had the first four horses already blanketed and tucked into their stalls munching on hay.

I felt a mixture of elation and pride as I looked at our new charges, all so different and all so full of potential.

"It's really happening," Lorne said dreamily, and Julie reached over and hugged his arm, resting her head on his shoulder for a moment.

"Despite his leg, I really like that bay and white guy," she said, smiling.

"There's a good chance he'll come sound," Lorne said. "But it might not improve completely in looks. He's not a great resale project with a blemish like that. People will be scared off by it."

"Well, maybe we'll have to keep him around for a while then," Julie said, laughing. She had a thing for pintos. Nipper had been her personal horse back when she still rode, and I knew she preferred horses with a lot of chrome over plain ones.

"Don't get too attached," Lorne warned. "They're all for sale. All of them."

He didn't look at me as he said this, but I felt the weight of his words none the less. Both Ace and Dragon were technically sales horses, although Lorne hadn't mentioned selling either of them in a while. But once Ace was going well under saddle, there might always be the possibility that someone would want to adopt him.

Dragon I knew was worth keeping around and improving because her value would increase exponentially the more she was worked with, especially once Chloe got some show miles under her belt.

But Ace was a different type of horse, a sweet, kind but maybe not quite as impressive-looking horse. There was only so much more money he was going to be worth to someone. With his small stature and unremarkable colouring, he wasn't ever going to be much over a four-figure horse, although he was already worth so much more to me.

There was always the dream in the back of my mind that if I *did* manage to survive for a few more years that I would someday find a way to buy him.

That is, if no one else stepped up to adopt him first.

"I don't know what it is about you girls getting all sentimental over these horses," Lorne went on, still in lecture mode. "They are working animals with a job to do and it's best not to forget that."

"Oh, really?" Chloe said, arching an eyebrow at him. "So, you're not attached to Bear there? You seem to have kept him around for quite a while for some reason. How old is he now? Like thirty?"

"Well, that's different," Lorne said gruffly. "Bear is ..." he broke off and cleared his throat. "Well, he ... okay, that's enough chit-chat. Didn't you say there was going to be some sort of lunch? I'm starving."

We ended up having an impromptu picnic at the barn. Julie took Adie up to the house to help her make sandwiches for everyone. And Nicholas, Chloe, and I brought out some hay bales into the aisle for seats so we could eat while watching the new horses.

Julie and Adie arrived with a picnic basket bulging with food. Sandwiches, chips and cookies, and thermoses of hot chocolate and coffee.

The racehorses were probably used to a bustling aisle crowded with people from their life at the track. But Bear and Nipper were excited by all the activity, and Nipper kept his eye fixed greedily on me the whole time. Bobbing his nose up and down and making faces while he begged me for whatever food I had in my hands.

Lorne kept getting up from his hay bale and walking up and down the aisles to look into the stalls of his new horses, his expression full of pride and happiness.

"Yes, the one with the big ears and the chestnut will be for Jeremy," Lorne muttered to himself. "that will do nicely."

"Hey!" Chloe said, overhearing, "I didn't know we were handing them out yet. What am I going to ride?"

"You already have Dragon to work with, Chloe. And we'll set you up with the grey. And maybe the black filly once she settles in. You won't be able to handle much more if you're not living here this summer. Not on top of chores and your obligations at home."

"Of course I can," Chloe said angrily. "And I didn't say that I wasn't going to live here for sure. I'm still working on it with my parents."

"Well, we need to plan as if you're not then," Lorne said firmly. "There will be more horses in the future, Chloe. I hope. But if Jeremy is coming all this way then he's going to need some solid projects. Right?"

"I suppose," Chloe muttered. She stood up abruptly and went over to stare moodily at the grey horse, frowning as she ran her gaze over his body.

I'd known from the beginning that I probably wasn't going to be given one of the new horses to ride. At least, not right away. Chloe and Jeremy were much more experienced than me, and I already had Nipper and Ace to ride. Still, I couldn't help feeling the tiniest bit left out.

"What about Bree?" Nicholas said, guessing my thoughts.

"Don't worry about me," I said quickly, irritated that he'd turned the attention my way. "I have lots to keep me busy."

"As for Bree and Adie," Lorne went on, "I was thinking that they could work together on rehabbing that spotty horse. We won't know much until our vet takes a look at him, but I'm guessing he'll need some sort of paddock rest and then slow hand-walking. You girls could do that, right?"

"Of course," I said quickly. "We'll do anything to help."

The party broke up as soon as the food was gone. Chloe headed home, deciding not to stay over another night.

She didn't say much when she left, and I was worried that her nose was still a little out of joint because she didn't get first pick of the horses.

CHAPTER 14

BREE

*T*hat afternoon, once everything had settled down, I had my first real ride on Nipper in the ring since December. We'd been trail riding as much as we could over the winter, but I'd wanted to wait until the entire ring was thawed before I had a lesson on him.

He was so excited that he could barely stand still at the mounting block. And he was off and moving at a brisk walk even before I'd settled in the saddle.

"Calm down, you," I told him, turning him in wide circles. Julie hadn't made it to the ring yet and I was supposed to be warming him up before our lesson.

Nipper jigged and snorted. His ears were pricked forward so hard that the tips were almost meeting in the middle.

I might as well let him go, I thought with a sigh of resignation. *There's no point fighting with him.*

"All right, Nipper, trot on."

That was enough for him. He broke into a fast trot with his

nose in the air and his front legs shooting out like he was one of those trotting racehorses that pulled the carts. But I left him alone and as soon as he reached the first corner his nose dropped and his rhythm became more balanced and respectable.

I asked him for circles and loops and direction changes, letting him move forward at his own pace but channeling his energy. I wasn't nervous at all. Nipper was forward but he wasn't a spooky or a naughty horse, and it was exhilarating to feel all that power rocketing us along.

We always lumped Nipper in with the senior horses, but he wasn't actually old. He'd been Julie's dressage horse before the accident, and he had been well schooled. He knew way more than I did, that was for sure.

"Wow, Bree, he's looking great," Julie said, ducking through the fence instead of using the gate.

I brought him down to a walk so I could catch my breath. Nipper wasn't breathing hard at all, but my lungs were having trouble keeping up with him.

He's so much different than riding Ace, I thought. Nipper was like riding on top of a powerful, flowing river while Ace had felt choppy and like he wasn't really going anywhere.

I pushed my disloyal thought hastily away. Of course, Nipper was going to feel more forward and fun than Ace. I was sure that once Ace was trained, he wouldn't feel so much like I was riding him through molasses. He was just a baby after all.

"All right," Julie said, rubbing her hands together gleefully. "Now that you've caught your breath, are you ready to get to work? I think we need to get the two of you out to a show or two this summer."

"On Nipper?" I asked in surprise. I'd never even thought of competing with him. I'd only had a show with Ace on my wish-list.

"Of course, why not?" she said. "You ride him beautifully and I have great, secret plans in mind for you."

She looked so excited that I couldn't help but laugh.

"Sure, I could do that," I said, reaching down to scratch Nipper's neck. "If you'll come and coach us."

It looked like my wish-list was expanding day by day. If it got any longer than I'd *have* to stay alive.

That night's dinner felt almost like a party. Lorne and Julie fired up the BBQ and made us all steaks. Nicholas had gone to the grocery store and bought us mounds of potato salad, chips and dip, and two types of pies for dessert.

I should have gone with him, but I'd sent Adie instead at the last minute, saying that I had to stay home and get started on my blog.

It was true that I did have a lot of work to do but really, I just wanted to avoid being alone with him. It was silly, I knew that, but for my own sanity I had to keep a little bit of distance from him. He would be going back to classes in a day or so and then I probably wouldn't see or hear from him until after school was over for the year.

We all stayed up late after dinner watching a movie and eating popcorn. At the last minute, just before the movie was over, I managed to sneak off to bed before everyone else, again avoiding any awkward goodnights with Nicholas.

I wasn't tired, though. I sat on my bed and kept myself from thinking about anything uncomfortable by working on my blog far into the night.

I'd caught some amazing photos of the horses, although the little black mare looked terrified in practically every single picture. It was hard to choose only a handful of them to use.

All our followers are going to love the spotted horse, I thought, *he's so striking.*

I worked far into the night, laying everything out so it was just right, and when I hit *publish,* I felt an exhausted thrill of plea-sure run through me.

I had done it. The October Horse's project had truly begun.

I sent Angelika a message with a link to the blog so she would be the very first one to read it. And then I slid happily under the covers, not even blinking once before I fell into a deep, contented sleep.

CHAPTER 15

BREE

*T*he next morning, I woke up feeling sore all over but in a good way. It was the kind of ache that came not after mindless, grueling physical labour like the type I'd been doing all winter, but by doing something athletic that you loved. My body was sore from my great ride on Nipper, and my mind was tired from all the writing and editing. I couldn't have been happier.

The sun streamed through my window and the smell of fresh coffee and bacon rose up the stairs.

I could hear muffled laughter downstairs, and then the front door thudded. I sat up with an involuntary smile on my face.

I hurriedly brushed my teeth and got dressed. My hair had grown out enough to be at that annoying stage where it was barely long enough to put in a ponytail. With a lot of effort, I could get an elastic around it but the whole thing would disintegrate the second I moved my head. Settling for a quick brush and a headband I headed out into the hall.

"Well, I can't say I like the short notice," Julie was saying as I walked toward the kitchen. "That doesn't say much for his character."

"Oh, I'm sure it was just a miscommunication," Lorne said patiently, and I entered the kitchen to see him sitting at the big wooden table with Chloe, Adie, and Nicholas. "It's not easy organizing things from overseas."

Nicholas caught my eye as I stood in the doorway and smiled in a way that made my heart stutter a little in my chest. The exact opposite of the way a heart was supposed to react to someone who was just a friend.

"You're finally up," he said as I made a beeline for the coffee maker.

"I stayed up half the night writing," I said. "What time is it anyway? You're here early, Chloe."

"I should have just stayed over," Chloe said. "But I jumped in the car the second Lorne called me."

She bounced up and down in her seat a little, nearly spilling her coffee. She wasn't in grubby riding clothes for once. She had on dark jeans and a fluttery, low-cut shirt. Her hair hung down to her shoulders in a neat wave and I was fairly sure she was wearing makeup. "I'm so excited."

"Excited about what?" I asked, looking around at everyone in bewilderment.

"Jeremy-from-Scotland, of course. He's here. Or at least he will be here this afternoon. He's arriving today. I can't wait to finally meet him."

"Today? I thought he wasn't coming for another week."

"Yes, that's what he told us," Julie said, pressing her lips together in a disapproving line. "That was the plan. I don't love these last-minute changes."

"Oh, I think it's perfect timing," Chloe said dreamily. "He'll be able to start with the horses right away."

She had clearly already forgiven him for getting the chestnut and the bay instead of her.

"Yes, but I'm running Lorne to the eye doctor this afternoon and you know those things hardly ever go on time. And then the vet is coming to look at the pinto's horse's leg. The timing is not ideal."

"Oh, I'll go pick him up," Chloe said quickly. "It should be me anyway. He'll want it to be a horse person to meet him and show him the ropes."

"Well, we're all horse people here, aren't we?" I asked, raising an eyebrow.

"Yes, of course," she said quickly, "but you're more into writing and *playing* with the horses rather than competing, right? It's totally different than being a professional."

"Are you a professional now?" I said, teasing her. Last week, she had been talking about giving up horses completely next year and going to University.

"Besides, Bree works just as hard as you do. Harder, actually," Nicholas said, raising an eyebrow.

"Oh, I didn't mean she didn't work hard," Chloe said hurriedly, her cheeks flushing, "but it's not like Bree is into eventing like Lorne and I are and, well, like Jeremy is. It's not the same level of riding."

"Since when was the October Horses about eventing?" Julie asked, staring at Chloe over her coffee. "I'm pretty sure it's about finding these horses good homes. No matter what the discipline. Right?"

"It is," Chloe said quickly, "of course it is. This is coming out all wrong. I just want Jeremy to feel as at home as possible here, that's all. He's coming to a whole new country all alone after all, and I thought it might be nice for him to meet someone who knows all about him and has so much in common with him. I really think we have a bond."

Suddenly, her weird attitude all made sense. I started to laugh and then so did Julie.

"Uh huh, I see," Julie said, her eyes shining, "and I suppose this has nothing to do with your unhealthy obsession with his rugged good looks, does it?"

"No!" Chloe protested. "I'm just trying to … Oh for pity's sake, I was just trying to make the guy feel welcome."

"That's very *welcoming* of you," Nicholas said, starting to laugh, too.

"I just meant … Oh fine. Why don't we all just go if it's such a big deal then."

"Now that is an excellent idea," Julie said, grinning at Chloe. "A proper welcoming committee is just the right thing to make him feel at home. You can take my car since it's big enough to fit everyone. Just be on your best behaviour, all of you, and try not to traumatize the poor guy on his first day. He'll book the first flight back out of here."

With that argument finally settled, we fell to devouring the bacon, eggs, and toast that Julie and Adie had made.

I felt a little guilty that my sleep-in day had meant that Julie had to do all the early morning feeds and cook us breakfast. It really was a good thing Jeremy was coming to help out. Adie and I got days off, but Julie never did. It didn't seem fair somehow.

"I did some thinking about the turnout schedule," Julie said, setting her cup of coffee down. "I think we should put the little black mare out with the senior horses in the field down below the barn. It's had a little chance to dry up. She is so timid. They might help her to come out of her shell.

"I'll put Nipper, Dragon, and Ace out in the pasture by the ring, and the rest of the new horses can take turns going into the smaller paddocks until we see what they're like with other horses. They're still not settled completely, and I don't want anyone to get hurt. It's too nice of a day for them to be cooped up inside, though. Especially after their long trip."

"What about the spotty horse?" Adie asked. "Is he staying inside?"

"I think so. At least until we can have the vet look at him. That injury does not look nice at all. We'll make sure there's another horse inside to keep him company."

Julie and Adie stayed back to do the dishes and tidy the kitchen, and the rest of us trooped down to the barn.

We were greeted by a chorus of impatient nickers the second we rolled back the door.

The moment she caught sight of Chloe, Dragon began to bang her hoof loudly and rhythmically against the wall of her stall.

"Oh, stop that, princess," Chloe said, rolling her eyes. "You've barely finished breakfast. You can't be that desperate to go outside."

Dragon pinned her ears at the group of us and tossed her nose up and down. She hated any disruption to her routine and having all these strange horses show up all of a sudden had pushed her over the edge into a simmering bad temper.

"I call not taking her out," I said quickly. "Here, Nicholas. Why don't you take Ace and I'll take Nipper? Dragon might be better if we lead them all out together."

"Don't make a fuss about her and she'll give it up," Lorne said, waving a hand airily in her direction. But that was easy for him to say since he wasn't the one handling her. The rest of us had come up with some pretty solid strategies about how to maneuver her when she was in a bad mood. She could be legitimately scary at times.

But although she did a bit of prancing, snorting, and head-shaking at the new horses, by the time she was outside, she settled down into a steady march. Only her tail fanning the air over her back marked how excited she really was.

We let Chloe put her out first, and the halter had barely cleared the top of the mare's ears before she spun away and galloped off into the distance, bellowing war cries at the top of her lungs.

"Do you think she'll jump the fence?" Nicholas asked, looking after her with wide eyes.

"That is a definite possibility," I said, shrugging. "Dragon pretty much does whatever she likes." I motioned for him to lead Ace out into the pasture ahead of me. Nipper was a little excited, but Ace just stood there, looking around with mild interest. And when his halter was taken off, he put his head down and began to graze. Not even looking excited to be outside at all.

Nipper took off at a brisk trot once he was free and, after a moment's hesitation, Ace sauntered after him.

"I'm not so sure about your horse, Bree," Chloe said, laughing, "he doesn't seem to have much spark."

"He has a perfect amount of spark," I said firmly, "you're just used to constant fireworks. Any horse would seem boring after Dragon."

Secretly I wondered, though. Ace was a much different horse than Nipper and, despite Julie's assurances that he was fine, I was a little worried that he might be something actually wrong with him. Maybe that's why he didn't seem to have much energy or motivation.

Lorne had already put out most of the seniors by the time we got back, but he'd left Bear inside.

"I figure he'll be good company for that pinto horse until we figure out what to do. Hopefully, the vet says he doesn't need months of stall rest. I hate to do that to them. Horses don't do well cooped up for too long."

He looked around, his eyes bright with happiness. There was nothing Lorne liked better than bossing around a barn full of people and horses. Delegating was practically his favourite thing.

"Chloe, you put that grey horse out first, he looks like a reliable citizen. And then put the little black mare out with the seniors, if you don't mind. The chestnut and the one with the big ears can go out next to the grey. You and Nicholas could take those ones out, Bree."

"You know, the horses probably have actual names," Chloe

said over her shoulder as she walked the grey down the aisle. "Or at least they used to. We could call this one Nugget."

"Well, you name them whatever you like," Lorne laughed. "I don't think they'll care much what they're called as long as somebody keeps feeding them."

"Nugget sounds good," I said. "But what about the others? Do you think we should let Jeremy name his own?"

"Oh, I doubt he'll care what they're called, either," Lorne said. "You go ahead, Bree. You're the media girl. Pick something people will like. Something they'll want to buy. And there's nothing saying that it has to have anything to do with their registered names, either."

"I kind of like keeping some link to their registered names," I said slowly. "It worked for Dragon and Ace."

"Well, you suit yourself."

"This one should be Rabbit with those ears," Nicholas said, staring in at Run Rabbit Run.

"Yeah, I like that, too." I picked up the bay's halter and leaned over the door beside Nicholas.

The horse stared at us with wide eyes, grabbed a mouthful of hay, and paced a rapid lap around his stall before stopping at his hay net again.

He didn't seem like the most relaxed type of guy and I suddenly felt a little out of my element handling this large, strange horse all by myself. But I couldn't say that in front of Lorne or Nicholas.

"Um, if you want to get the chestnut, we can lead them out together," I said, trying to sound like I knew what I was doing. "I mean, as long as you're comfortable handling him."

Nicholas had grown up here, but he wasn't really a horsey guy. I didn't want him to get trampled.

"I think I still know what I'm doing, Bree," he said, laughing as he walked away. "I was riding before I could walk. I just outgrew it, that's all."

"How can someone outgrow horses?" I shook my head, truly baffled. "That concept doesn't even make sense."

"You know, there are other things besides horses …"

"Nope." I held up a hand. "No crazy talk like that in the barn. You'll offend them."

"Yes, boss," Nicholas said with a grin, disappearing toward the next stall.

"Good boy, Rabbit," I said softly, rolling back the door and stepping inside. "You want to go out to your paddock with your friends, right?"

His eyes bulged wide, and he held his breath when I touched him. His banana ears snapped forward and locked on me in a way that was both funny and terrifying. Suddenly, he reached out and nudged me on the arm with his nose. Hard.

"Ow," I said, stepping back. "Okay, I get it. You don't know me, and you have no idea where you are or what's going to happen. But you're safe here, I promise. Now let's just put your halter on."

I held the halter gingerly toward him and his eyes bulged again. He sucked in a deep breath and shot his head way up into the air with his nose as far as it could go, trying to avoid me touching his face at all costs. He tilted his head so one rolling eye could stare down at me, but otherwise, he kept his nose tipped toward the ceiling.

"Wow, that is so not helpful," I told him, starting to laugh. "You know you look ridiculous, right? How am I supposed to get you outside with your friends like that?"

"Will this help?" Nicholas, holding the lead of the relaxed-looking chestnut, stood outside Rabbit's stall with an apple in his hand.

"Maybe. Thanks. It's worth a try."

It turned out that food was definitely the key to this horse's heart. Rabbit's oversized ears shot forward and he dove for the apple, nearly knocking it out of my hand. He kept his nose down while he crunched it happily, green and white drool running down his chin.

I took the opportunity to wrestle the halter onto his head.

"I've never seen a horse do that before," I said, patting the big animal's neck. Now that the halter was on, he just stood there with his head hanging like the whole thing had never happened.

Nicholas laughed and we headed out together into the sunshine where the grey horse, Nugget, was already busy exploring his little paddock. Chloe had her elbows resting on the fence and was watching him with a half-smile on her face.

I was glad; she looked happier to be working with him. She hadn't really seemed too impressed when Lorne had said that this was the horse she was supposed to ride.

"He's a nice, solid little guy," she said, as if guessing my thoughts, "and he has a fun personality. I think he'll do all right."

She turned and sighed, looking over at the chestnut. "So, what are you planning to call that one? TeaBag? Tea Time?"

"How about just Time? Or Timely?"

"Timely does have a nice ring to it. Yeah, that sounds good."

Rabbit and the chestnut, now Timely, trotted around their paddocks a few times, snorting and squealing at each other in excitement. I wondered if they'd even met each other before their long trailer ride to Canada.

I made sure to take a few more photos of their first day outside so I could do some social media updating later.

Turning out the little black mare didn't go quite so smoothly, though. She'd planted her front feet as soon as Chloe had gotten her near the pasture gate. And then she'd reared, ripped the rope out of Chloe's hands and bolted back into the barn as fast as she could go. Her hooves clattered all the way down the aisle as she fled directly back to her stall.

"What the heck?" Chloe said, looking down at the small rope burn on her palm. "What was that?"

We found the little mare in the back of her stall shaking hard, her rolling eyes white around the edges.

"You know, maybe let's leave her in for today," Lorne said, frowning at the terrified horse. "Give her another day to get settled. Once she calms down, we'll get one of you to brush her and make friends with her. She looks pretty overwhelmed."

"Poor thing," Chloe said, going in and carefully taking off the filly's halter. The mare didn't even move when Chloe stepped away. It was like she was locked in place, her whole body still shaking.

We brought her some fresh hay and even shook a little grain into her bucket to encourage her out of her corner. She wasn't having any of it, though. She didn't even acknowledge that we were there.

Once we went away and stopped hovering over her, it still took her another five minutes before she finally stepped forward on her own and began to eat.

CHAPTER 16

BREE

The airport where Jeremy's plane was set to land was about an hour away. Nicholas drove his mother's ancient blue SUV, which had plenty of room for all of us plus for whatever amount of luggage Jeremy decided to bring.

Chloe sat excitedly in the back seat with Adie, clutching a hand-written cardboard sign that had *Welcome to Canada* on it in bold, red marker. Underneath that was Jeremy's name. I was just glad she hadn't added any hearts or flowers to it.

"What?" she'd asked when I'd raised my eyebrows. "This is how you welcome international visitors. Don't you watch movies at all?"

She had a point. This was the first international visitor I'd ever picked up from the airport. What did I know?

"Come on, let's get some coffee and donuts so we can welcome him properly," Nicholas said, detouring through the drive-through without waiting for any of us to answer. It was a given that none of us was going to turn down pastries any time soon.

"You people are totally corrupting me," Adie said ten minutes later, working her way through an apple fritter. "We never had this type of food when I was growing up. It was mostly natural, organic, sugar-free stuff."

"Terrible," Chloe said, shaking her head. "You poor deprived child."

"It wasn't all bad," Adie said quickly, never too interested in saying bad things about her family. "My parents are really good cooks and they taught us all sorts of great recipes. Eating food that you've grown yourself from the garden is pretty amazing."

"Uh huh," Chloe said, "whatever you say."

"Besides, we were allowed to have sugary treats on our birthdays and holidays."

"Adie, that's practically criminal. What a way to grow up."

"Well, there were ten of us, including my parents, so it wasn't as bad as it could have been. That's a lot of birthdays and holidays in a year."

Nicholas put his blinker on and eased the car into the right lane, following the sign that led to the airport.

"I'm so excited," Chloe said, bouncing up and down a little on her seat. "It's going to be so fun to have someone really competitive to train and event with."

"Yeah, yeah," I said, "you've mentioned that before. You'd better hope that one of the new horses will be able to keep up with Dragon."

"That's unlikely," she said confidently. "But Jeremy can get used to being a close second. Ooh, look at the plane."

We looked out the windows to see a huge jet just taking off, engines roaring as it launched into the air. The car windows rattled a little and my ears were full of the rush and roar of it.

I suddenly felt a pang of longing as I watched it rise up over our heads. I'd never given any thought to travel before, but now I wondered where I'd go if I had the chance. If I had the money, the lifespan, or the motivation to do something completely different with my life.

"Where would you go if you could just hop on a plane and fly anywhere?" I asked suddenly, turning to look at Nicholas.

His eyes widened in surprise and then he smiled.

"Um, the UK first, and then maybe Italy and France. After that, I'd like to explore Egypt. South America sounds good, too."

"I'd like to compete at Badminton," Chloe said dreamily. She stared off to the grassy hills beyond the runway, probably imagining her and Dragon soaring over some impossibly huge jump.

"I've always wanted to go to Africa," Adie said quietly. "My parents both volunteered at a health center in Zambia when they were young, that's actually how they met. I've always thought I'd like to see the place where they first fell in love."

"That's sweet," I said, turning around to look at her. "It would be pretty amazing to see all those elephants and tigers in real life. I've only seen them on television. I've haven't ever been to a zoo."

"Well, we'll have to put it on our future to-do list," Nicholas said casually. "Travel around the world together and make sure to get Bree to a zoo."

Chloe met my gaze and held it for a second, widening her eyes and then grinning.

I turned away quickly, looking out the window to hide my confusion.

Nicholas nonchalantly making future plans that included me was not something I wanted to think about right then.

There must have been a lot of people coming to the island on that particular weekend because the entire parking lot was packed with cars. It would be a miracle if we were able to find a spot at all. The lot was full of people circling around like sharks looking for a vacant space.

Most of them were probably snowbirds migrating west in the hopes of escaping worse winter weather than what we had had. I had complained a lot about our few months of snow, but it had been nothing compared to what was still happening in places like Saskatchewan or Yellowknife or Northern Ontario. Most of Canada was like an icefield well into March and beyond. Our island probably seemed like a tropical paradise to those people.

"How are we supposed to find him?" Chloe said, staring around at all the cars.

"We'll just go inside to the arrivals section and see if we can find anyone who looks like him," Nicholas said, suddenly plunging into a parking spot just as someone else was pulling out of it. "You have your sign anyway. I'm sure we'll find him eventually."

When it was finally time to go inside, we all filed into the packed lobby and then stood in a huddle off to one side as the crowd of arrivals marched past us.

"Do you see him?" Chloe asked, holding up her sign hopefully. But there was no sign of him.

"What about that guy?" Adie pointed at a short man in a knit cap and a dark green coat standing by the luggage carousel. He had the wiry look of someone used to spending their days on horseback, his boots could even have been paddock boots. But when he turned around, we saw that he was about twenty years older than the man we were looking for.

"Close," Chloe said, laughing and turning away to scan the crowd again. "He looks like he could be a rider but he's way too old. Keep looking."

"Hello, you're looking for Jeremy McFadden?" The man we'd been staring at had suddenly appeared right in front of us and was studying Chloe's sign with raised eyebrows.

"Um, yes?" Chloe said, her smile slipping a little bit. "Do you know him?"

"Yes, I know him very well," the man said in a thick, lilting accent that sounded almost musical. "He is *me*."

We all stared at him in confusion, not saying a word.

This man couldn't be Jeremy from Scotland. He looked nothing like the photos we'd seen online. This guy was older with a sharp, weathered face and bright blue eyes surrounded by deep lines. Despite the charming smile on his face, he had a slightly hardened expression as if he'd seen some trouble in his life. The curly hair poking out from under his blue knit hat was brown with sprinkles of white.

"I'm sorry, but you are definitely not Jeremy," Chloe said firmly, "you don't look a thing like the pictures."

"Pictures?" The man looked bewildered. "What pictures?"

"You know, your—" Chloe broke off abruptly. It wasn't like Jeremy-from-Scotland had actually sent a close-up glamour-shot of himself with his application. All the photos that Chloe had seen of him had been found when she was busy stalking him online. But there *had* been hundreds of photos on the internet, and they didn't look a thing like this guy. Had we somehow mixed him up?

Chloe's face and neck flushed a deep shade of red and for once, she was at a loss for words.

"I can assure you that I really am Jeremy McFadden. Here—" He reached into the back pocket of his pants and fished out a battered brown leather wallet. He flipped it open and held up his ID for us all to see. The photo was him all right and it said Jeremy James McFadden right there in bold writing. "I'm here to ride your horses."

"Well, welcome to Canada," Nicholas said after an embarrassing pause. "We're happy to have you here. Let me help you with your bags."

"Ah, no need. I travel light." Jeremy had been eyeing up the luggage carousel where bags and cases were being moved by the automatic conveyer belt in rapid circles. He suddenly darted forward and grabbed the strap of a large, battered-looking brown duffle bag that looked like it had seen better days. It had patches sewn all over it in the shape of different flags and crests. Probably souvenirs from his travels around the world.

"This is me all set," he said, looking at us expectantly. "I'm starving. When do we eat? You don't have a casino around here, do you? I could kill for a beer to unwind."

We looked at each other in bewilderment. Did people just pop by casinos for drinks in Scotland?

"Um, I have no idea," I said finally. "I've never even been to one. We could look it up, though."

"Never mind, another time. My second choice is to get back to the farm and get some sleep."

It was a strange ride home. Chloe didn't say another word, leaving the rest of us to try and make stilted conversation. I think we were all a little in shock with the way things were turning out.

We'd been expecting another fun, young working student, and now we were stuck with this old guy all summer, maybe longer. And if he wasn't the Jeremy McFadden that we'd seen all the competition photos of, then who on earth was he?

If he sensed our confusion and disappointment, he didn't show it. He spent the rest of the ride polishing off our box of muffins and donuts one by one. And drinking the lukewarm coffee we'd saved back for him.

When I glanced back, I almost thought I saw him pouring a splash of something into his coffee from a little bottle that he'd pulled out of his jacket.

What on earth are Lorne and Julie going to say when they see him? I thought anxiously. *And what on earth are we supposed to do with him? Can he even ride?*

Our stilted conversation died away completely when we reached the long driveway to the farm.

Jeremy leaned forward eagerly to take in the view, but there was a certain tension in his mouth and around his eyes. A hardening of his expression that made me think that he was not quite as sure of his reception as he pretended to be.

"Should we stop at the barn to meet the horses first?" Nicholas asked uncertainly, glancing over at me.

I started to agree. One of us could run up to the house and prepare Julie and Lorne ahead of time rather than throwing Jeremy completely into the fire. It was true he wasn't quite as advertised, but that wasn't really his fault. We were the ones who had made a mistake.

"Oh, no, I think we should go *right* to the house and have him meet Lorne and Julie first thing," Chloe said in a hard voice. She clearly still wasn't over her disappointment that he wasn't *the* Jeremy McFadden she'd been expecting.

We might as well get it over with, I thought.

Lorne and Julie were in the kitchen when we trooped inside, and the air smelled like fresh baking.

Julie had said something earlier about how it must be intimidating for young Jeremy to have come so far from halfway across the world. She'd been worried that he was going to miss his mother.

I somehow didn't think it would be a problem now.

"Hello," I called, and Julie appeared in the kitchen doorway. She scanned our faces eagerly and then I saw her expression flicker with confusion as she locked on Jeremy.

"Er, hello?" she said, keeping her polite expression fixed in place.

"Um, mom, this is Jeremy," Nicholas said, looking at her meaningfully. "Jeremy from Scotland."

"Ah, is he?" Julie said, her eyes widening. "That's … it's nice to meet you. Um, well, come in."

Lorne was in the middle of helping himself to a cinnamon bun when we all filed slowly into the kitchen.

"Welcome to October Horses," he said glancing up at Jeremy. "Pull up a seat and help yourself. You'll probably want to have a little break before you meet the horses. How long was that plane ride, anyway?"

"Over a day and a half in the air. More than enough for me," Jeremy said with a laugh. He shrugged his duffle bag off one shoulder and let it drop to the kitchen floor with a solid thud. "I'd kill for a coffee. And I need a bathroom. I have to pee like a racehorse."

Julie's eyes widened. "Down the hall to the right," she said in a tense voice.

As soon as the bathroom door had closed behind him, Julie rounded on us. "Who on earth *is* he?" she hissed.

"He really is Jeremy McFadden," Nicholas whispered. "He showed us his ID."

"He's a liar," Chloe said angrily. "He's probably a criminal of some sort. He came here under false pretenses."

"Did he?" Nicholas asked. "Did he actually lie on his application or did we just assume who he was? What age did he put down?"

"Oh," Julie stopped. "We didn't actually ask the candidates for their ages, I suppose. We just said that they had to be over eighteen."

"But all those competitions he wrote down," Chloe insisted. "They were all the same ones the other Jeremy had done and won. He had to be lying about those then."

"Lots of people compete at those events," Lorne said. "He looks like he's spent time in the saddle. I think it's just a misunderstanding on our part."

"It isn't," Chloe insisted. "He misled us on purpose. There's something shifty about him."

"He had good references," Julie said reluctantly. "But I can't say I like the look of him, either. We can't have him staying upstairs with the girls. What would Adie's parents say if we let a middle-aged man sleep two-doors down from her."

"I think they'd have more to worry about if he really were a twenty-year old boy," Nicholas said, laughing.

"My parents always say we should look for the good in everyone. And I think he seems nice enough," Adie said. "I'm not bothered by him sleeping upstairs."

"Still, it wouldn't be appropriate for him to live in the house. He'll have to sleep in the barn."

"He can't sleep in the barn, it's freezing," I protested. Even the idea of it made me shiver with cold.

"Well, he can't—"

Julie broke off as Jeremy came sauntering out of the bathroom, whistling a little tune under his breath.

"I'd love that cup of coffee now, love," he said to her, grinning in a way that made me think he'd overheard the whole conversation.

Julie grimaced but she went and got the coffee pot and splashed black coffee into the mug that he held out. He probably wasn't going to be able to get away with calling her *love* more than once.

Lorne had been uncharacteristically quiet, but now he studied Jeremy openly, taking in the man's whip-thin frame and tanned skin.

"You've been riding horses all your life?" he asked, taking a sip of his own coffee.

"Since I was a blip in my mother's belly," Jeremy said with a laugh. "All the McFaddens ride. You've probably heard of my cousin young Jeremy. Arrogant little mutt but he's destined for the Olympics at some point, I suppose. He has just that kind of luck."

Ahh, a nod of understanding went around the room and

everyone, but Chloe, relaxed a little. So that explained it then. At least partly.

"My family has run the Glenbrittle Stud for the last two hundred years. My brothers and sister run it now. Mostly steeplechasers but we dabble in others."

"Why don't you run it yourself?" Chloe said rudely.

"Ah, well, there are six of us so that's a little too many hands on the rudder, if you see what I'm saying. Besides, I don't like the idea of staying in one place all my life. I like to see new things and new places. And horses are the same the world over."

"Where have you travelled to?" Adie asked shyly.

"All over. This is my first time in Canada, though. One of the most interesting places I've ever been was in South Africa. I did a stint at a game reserve, helping to break in their ponies."

"Well, you'll probably want to meet the horses and get settled," Lorne said thoughtfully. Julie sent him a warning look that he ignored.

"Yep, just show me where to drop my things and a place to have a nap. I can get to work right after that," Jeremy said. "I'm itching to stretch my legs."

"Right, well, I was thinking that maybe you could take the second bedroom in my house," Lorne said, ignoring Julie's yelp of protest. "There's lots of room and I wouldn't mind having a hand around the cottage from time to time."

"Well, that sounds just fine," Jeremy said, "you lead the way. Maybe we could share a drink after dinner and we can go over this summer's show schedule. You don't know if there's a casino in the area, do you?"

Julie made some ominous muttering noises under her breath, but there was no stopping Lorne once he'd made up his mind.

CHAPTER 17

BREE

*J*ulie had already brought the new horses in from their paddocks, and they were tucked in their stalls working on piles of hay.

I walked down the barn aisle, trailing a little behind everyone else, delighting in the sounds of our new houseguests rustling in their stalls, and occasionally splashing in their water buckets and nickering to their neighbours.

It's hard to believe this is really happening, I thought, hugging myself in delight.

Even if Jeremy was a disappointment, at least we'd made a start. Eventually he'd move on and we'd get new working students. And this time, we'd be better at the application process.

Jeremy looked around the barn with interest, studying the horses with a look that was hard to interpret.

"I thought you might like to work with this chestnut here and the bay," Lorne said.

Chloe made a strangled, choking noise under her breath and disappeared into the tack room.

"This chestnut is a good one," Jeremy said, pausing in the horse's doorway and running an appraising eye over him. "But the bay most likely won't make a jumper."

"You can't possibly know that," Chloe said, sticking her head furiously back into the aisle. "You haven't even seen him move. You can't dismiss him like that. You don't know anything about him."

"True," Jeremy said, completely unperturbed. "And I've occasionally been wrong in the past. But I've seen a lot of horses in my life, and I get a good sense of them right away. This one will want to keep his feet on the ground."

Chloe snorted and rolled her eyes.

"Well, should we take the chestnut out to the ring and put him through his paces?" Lorne asked, his eyes fixed on Jeremy. "Let's lunge him and see what you think of him."

At that, Chloe stomped right out of the barn and we heard her car roar to life.

She was really not having a good weekend.

The pinto horse nickered under his breath as I came near and pricked his ears, sticking his head right over his door and dipping his head down to search my pockets.

"Well, you're sure friendly," I told him, scratching behind his ears and arranging his thick black forelock neatly in the middle of his forehead. "What are we going to call you? Boots or Chilly?"

He snorted and then reached over and rubbed his nose on my arm.

"Do you like the name Chilly? I can see myself calling you that. But those are some mighty fine white boots you're wearing."

His strange stockings came right up over his knees and almost to his armpits on the front. Jagged white markings crossed his shoulder so that the dark bay patch on his chest stood out boldly like a shield in front of him.

Too bad his injured leg looked so awful. I peered over the stall door to look at the curved bulge at the back of his leg.

"He seems to be a nice boy," Julie said, coming up behind me. "Shame about that leg. The vet should hopefully be here soon. With any luck we can get the ultrasound done today and get an idea of how bad the damage is. I already left a message for Eddie to see if we can get access to whatever diagnostics they've done already. If any. That looks like a pretty recent injury and we shouldn't waste much time before getting it treated."

"He will get better though, right?" I asked, not liking the dark look on her face.

She shrugged. "Hopefully. He's got a good chance anyway. But I'm going to bet the vet will say he needs stall rest for a while. And then probably he won't be able to go into full pasture turnout right away. We'll have to figure out a smaller paddock for him. It really limits his potential adopters, though. Not everyone wants to take on a horse with a past injury. And the swelling on his leg might not ever go away, even if he becomes fully sound."

"Aw, poor guy."

"It doesn't mean his life is over. We're going to give him as much of a chance as we can."

The vet came not long after that and it was just as Julie had suspected.

Chilly was to be on stall rest for at least a month, and maybe longer. He would need to be cold-hosed and have his legs wrapped daily and later, when the vet said it was okay, he was to be hand-walked for increasing periods of time. He would be on anti-inflammatories to take down the swelling and take away some of the pain.

"He's a decent-looking horse," the vet said, patting Chilly on his arched neck, "and you never know, he might come out of it sound. At least enough to make a good trail horse for someone. Time will tell."

Adie and I watched carefully while Julie showed us how to properly poultice and then bandage the gelding's front legs. He was to be mostly our responsibility from then on, so we had to know what we were doing.

"Right," Julie said, nodding approvingly as we got him settled back in his stall. "Now that he's taken care of, it's time to get the two of you organized. Adie, let's pop you on Nipper later this afternoon and see how you do with him. Bear is a great boy, but he's not up to much hard work. Time to get your riding education started properly. And Bree, you could ride Ace at the same time. I'll give you a bit of a lesson together."

I broke into a smile but when I looked over at Adie, she looked less than thrilled. In fact, she almost looked terrified.

The rest of the day was pretty non-eventful after that dramatic morning.

I kept busy with chores and it wasn't until the afternoon that Nicholas caught me alone.

"Hey," he said, finding me in Ace's stall where I was giving the little gelding a good grooming before our lesson. "I'm glad I found you."

"Oh, hey," I said, as casually as I could. "I guess you're heading back to school now."

"Yeah, I'd better head back so I can cram in some more studying. Exams are coming up fast. I'm looking forward to it being over."

He paused and then took a deep breath, leaning his elbows on the stall door and keeping his eyes fixed on Ace. "Look, Bree, I'm sorry I didn't call or text you much when I was away. I kind of wish I didn't have to leave …"

"Nicholas, it's okay," I said quickly, wanting to get this conversation over with as fast as possible. "I don't want you to stay. I mean, of course it's always great to have you around, but I don't want you to feel obligated to be here. You're busy at school and that's really what you need to focus on right now.

"You deserve to be happy, and you deserve to hang out with your friends. I don't want to get in the way of that."

"Hang out with my friends?" Nicholas said in confusion. "Well, you're my friend too, aren't you?"

The small bit of hope that had been stubbornly lodged in my chest fizzled and died a small, painful death. Nicholas didn't see me as anything more than that. He probably never had. He had moved on a long time ago.

"Yes," I said, fixing a determined smile on my face. "Exactly. We are just good friends. And I want the best for you. So, you don't need to worry about texting me or calling while you're away. You need to focus on school, and on your new ... friends there. You can't be in two places at once."

"Right," he said slowly, looking confused. "Well, I guess I'll be off then. I'll try and get home soon. Just to see how the new horses are getting on."

"Perfect," I said, keeping my smile fixed determinedly in place. "Have a good drive back. I'll see you when ... whenever I see you."

I didn't look up from running my comb repetitively through Ace's mane until I was sure he was gone.

Then I took a shuddering breath and leaned my forehead against the horse's warm neck.

That wasn't as bad as I thought it would be, I told myself. *Nicholas can go back to school without feeling obligated to spend all his time hanging out with the sick girl. And I still get to keep him as my friend.*

So, if it had gone so well then why did I feel so hollow inside? Why did I feel like I'd let something special slip away?

CHAPTER 18

ADIE

*D*ear Mom, today I learned that I completely suck as a rider. I always thought that I knew what I was doing when I was cantering Teddy around back home, but it turns out that I know nothing. And I want to come home.

I'm not sure why Nipper doesn't like me, but he doesn't. I know he's capable of being good. I see the way he is with Bree, but he's made it clear that he doesn't want me to ride him. And I agree with him.

Riding Bear was fun. Riding Nipper felt like I was about to die. I think I'm the most incompetent person on this property. Did I mention that I want to come home?

Oh, right, I forgot that there's no home to go back to. And also, did you know that your other kids are miserable? Did you know that Phil used to terrify me? And that he hit Grady? And that Grady is too scared to tell you about it. You probably don't know any of that because you never bothered to call me back. I've left like four messages for you.

I guess you don't care about any of us at all. Maybe you never did.

. . .

I tore the paper out of my notebook and crumpled the letter up into a tiny ball, tossing it into the garbage can. Tears stung my eyes.

It wasn't just my family that was bothering me. My first, and hopefully only, lesson on Nipper couldn't have gone worse. I would never get on him again as long as I lived if I could help it.

I lay back on my bed and stared up at the ceiling, going over my painful ride in my head for the hundredth time.

"Adie, you have to sit up," Julie had said, her voice laced with frustration. "I know being curled over like that feels safe, but it really isn't. You'll be way more secure once you relax and sit back."

"Okay," I'd told her, willing my tense muscles to release their grip. But they weren't at all convinced that riding Nipper was a good idea and, despite my efforts, I stayed hunched over, my fingers grabbing at the reins even though I didn't mean to pull on his mouth.

Right from the beginning, our ride had not started well. Nipper didn't stand quietly like Bear to be brushed and tacked up. Instead, he shifted around restlessly in the cross-ties, and pawed a front hoof against the concrete over and over.

And he'd nipped me sharply through my jacket when I'd gotten too close to his head.

He'd smartened up a little when Bree had come back into the barn. He stood at attention in the cross-ties and tossed his nose up and down when he saw her.

"Are you being a good boy?" she'd called to him as she'd headed toward Ace's stall. "Don't let him fool you, Adie. He's a big softy underneath that nippy exterior."

But as soon as she was gone, he'd started shifting around restlessly again.

I really wished I'd taken her up on her offer to help me tack him up. He'd always seemed so quiet when she was handling him that I assumed that he was always like that.

Things didn't get much better when I got to the ring. He'd practically pulled me there in the first place, and when I'd tried to stop him, he'd stepped on my foot. And I was pretty sure it hadn't been an accident.

"Are you all ready for this?" Julie had asked, beaming at us and patting Nipper fondly on the neck. He'd nickered to her under his breath and greedily taken the peppermint she'd offered him between his sharp teeth. "He's a lovely mover, much more forward than Bear of course, but then he isn't thirty years old. You'll love him."

I seriously had my doubts.

Nipper did stand still while I clambered up into his saddle. He was technically a little smaller than Bear in height, but he was wider and the way his neck arched and his back filled out under saddle, and the way his ears swiveled around alertly, made my stomach clench.

And I didn't feel much better when he stepped off smartly into a walk. It wasn't the steady amble of Bear or the long-remembered march of Teddy. This was a swinging, rocking motion like a boat at sea.

I squeaked and clutched the front of the saddle immediately. I guess I grabbed a handful of reins too, because Nipper tossed his head impatiently and yanked the leather through my fingers.

"Easy, there," Julie said, "okay, let's bring him to a halt and adjust your position."

But Nipper didn't want to halt. He scooted forward instead, and it was all I could do to turn him back to Julie with my heart in my throat.

"You're okay," Julie said, patting my leg and running her hand soothingly down Nipper's neck. "When you asked him to stop you clamped your legs against his sides. Did you feel that?"

"No." I shook my head and gulped.

"Okay, let's start over. We'll adjust your position and then I'll walk beside you. I know Nipper's stride feels different, but it's just like riding Bear."

It really wasn't but I nodded and let her adjust my legs into place and my fingers on the reins and my pelvis in the saddle. But I was only half-listening. The other part of my mind was just locked in fear. My palms were sweating and I could hardly breathe. I really just wanted to get off this horse.

"Does that make sense?" Julie said, and I nodded even though I hadn't heard anything she'd said.

It wasn't quite so bad with Julie walking beside us with her hand resting lightly on Nipper's inside rein. I could relax a little and take a few breaths at least.

But the second she stepped away, Nipper sped up and I could feel my anxiety spike. Nipper's ears flicked back at me and I knew he could sense how scared I was.

"That's it, just circle him around me here," Julie said, smiling at us encouragingly. "You're doing good."

It didn't feel good, though. I felt like I was going to vomit any moment. This wasn't like what riding Bear or Teddy had been like at all. Nipper might look like an adorable stuffed toy, but he felt like riding a loaded missile.

She had us change direction a few times, correcting my position and reminding me to relax and breathe. It must have looked better than it felt because pretty soon she was coming at me with the lunge-line in her hand.

"I think you're ready to do some trotting, don't you?"

No, I thought, feeling ill.

Julie was looking up at me so kindly that I didn't want to disappoint her by saying how I really felt. That I wanted to leap off Nipper and go back to Bear as fast as I could.

Out of the corner of my eye, I saw Bree leading Ace up to the ring. Nipper saw them at the same time and threw his head up in the air and let out a bugling neigh that shook his whole body.

I gasped and clutched the front of the saddle, trying to find anything to hold on to.

"What is up with you, Nipper?" Bree called out to him, laughing. "It's just us."

Nipper snorted again and then dropped his head, ripping the reins through my fingers so he could itch his nose on one stretched-out foreleg.

"I hope he's not giving you any trouble," Bree said, as she swung up on Ace and let him amble over to us. "He has a few tricks but he's a really good guy. I love riding him."

"Do you?" I asked doubtfully.

"Yes, of course," she said, giving me a funny look. "He's really fun. When you're friends with him, he'll totally take care of you."

I don't think we'll ever be friends, I thought skeptically, watching his pointy little ears swivel around to follow Bree as she rode Ace to the far end of the ring.

"All right, let's start him off in a walk again and then we can break into a trot."

I started to protest, but Nipper must have been listening to her because as soon as she said the word *trot,* he jolted forward. It probably wasn't a big movement, but I was turning to face Julie at the time and my balance was off. I slipped sideways and instead of catching myself I just kind of went with the motion and let myself fall. Anything was better than staying up there.

The ground was harder than I'd expected though, and I landed on my shoulder with a sharp thud before the rest of my body hit the ground. My breath *whooshed* out of me, and there was a terrifying moment when my lungs wouldn't work before the air rushed back into them again. I sat up, gasping.

"Oh my gosh, are you hurt? What happened? You just sort of slipped off there," Julie said, kneeling down beside me.

I rested my head on my knees, trying to assess if, and how badly, I was injured.

I was okay. There would be bruises, but nothing was broken.

I looked up at Julie to tell her that, and then realized that if I wasn't hurt then she'd want me to get back on right away. That's what horse people did. If you weren't injured, then you had to get back on. There was no way I wanted to finish that ride. I was never getting on Nipper again.

"My elbow," I said, picking the first body part that came to mind. I cupped my arm, gingerly, wincing in pain. "I think I pulled something."

"Uh oh, we should get some ice on it. We might have to run you down to emergency."

"Ah, it's not that bad," I said quickly. "I'm sure I just strained it. You're right about the ice, though. I'll go put some on right away."

I stood up, wincing for real this time as I felt the actual sore parts of my body begin to throb. I sent a sidelong glance at Nipper, who was standing tucked in behind Julie, his wide eyes innocently peeking over her shoulder at me. I could swear he was laughing.

I waved off Bree and Julie's concern and limped my way back to the house, feeling like the world's worst rider. Why had I frozen like that? Why couldn't I have just listened to Julie's instructions and done what she'd told me to do? Riding Bear and Teddy had never felt anything like being on Nipper. I'd never been terrified like that before.

When I was far enough up the hill away from the ring, I turned back to look down below. Bree was trotting Ace in happy, relaxed circles at one end of the ring and Julie was lunging Nipper down at the other.

From this distance, Nipper looked beautiful. Like a painted carousel horse cantering around with his neck arched.

I turned away again wondering why I was never quite good enough at anything.

CHAPTER 19

ADIE

That whole next week, nobody said another thing about me riding Nipper. I was given another lesson on Bear, and then given permission to take him on daily walks around the farm and on the short trails in front of the property.

I was so proud and happy that first day I got to go out. Bree came with us on Ace since Nipper was much too fast of a walker and would leave Bear in his dust in seconds.

Both horses moved at about the same pace, happy to saunter along in the sunshine, just enjoying the scenery.

"Ace, it's like you're a thirty-year-old horse, too," Bree laughed at him.

Our daily walks improved my confidence again and my bruises from my fall off Nipper began to fade.

I was getting more used to handling the horses on the ground, too. It used to be that I only felt confident leading the seniors in and out of the pasture. But now I happily handled Ace, Timely, and Nugget, too.

I could spend all day brushing our injured horse, Chilly. He loved the attention. He was getting a little bored and lonely with his stall rest and I'd taken to constructing new toys and treat-feeders for his stall. Anything to keep his mind off the fact that he was stuck inside.

The heat and swelling had left his leg after a few days of cold-hosing, medication, and bandaging, but the ugly curve in his tendon was still there.

Lately, I'd begun to spend time with the little black mare, Follow, too. She was able to go out on pasture with the other senior horses now, but she was still scared of everything.

Whenever anyone led her out of the barn, she would look for any opportunity to spook and snort at shadows or noises, or pretty much anything.

Most of the time, her spooks were small, but once in a while she would scare herself badly enough to spin and bolt back to her stall again. And if that happened, she would just stand and shake like she had on that first day, her muscles rock-hard and her eyes rolling. Her gaze fixed on something only she could see. When she got into that state, there was no point forcing her out of her stall again for the rest of the day.

"I think we should run some bloodwork on her," Julie said, "there is something not quite right about her. Maybe it's past trauma, but it's just as likely that it's something going on inside of her body. Or a combination of both, maybe."

I had taken to visiting with Follow after my grooming sessions with Chilly. And gradually, the little mare had started to get to know me.

She'd even nickered one afternoon when I'd brought her a carrot.

Finally, one day, Julie said that I might as well brush the mare, so I'd added her onto my list of horses to groom. I'd discovered that she loved being brushed more than anything, as long as you only used the softest of brushes.

I'd found a goat-hair brush that felt like a soft cloud to use against her silky coat. She would stand there with her eyes closed while I ran it over her sensitive sides.

But if I used anything harder, her eyes would shoot open and she'd rush cross her stall and stand in the far corner, shaking again.

"Poor girl," I'd croon to her, "good girl. You're okay, nobody is going to hurt you here."

All in all, my life at the farm was turning out to be much better than I'd originally hoped.

I liked everyone, even Jeremy, who was a bit odd and clearly had a chip on his shoulder. I was settling in so well that there were days at a time where I hardly thought about my family.

I'd gotten a few calls lately from Flora, but she only called at night when the rest of the family was busy and the details that she gave me about their life on the road were few and far between.

"Everything is fine. I just want to work on our song," she'd insist. Or she'd ask me to tell her all about the horses.

My songwriting was another thing that was going well. I worked on Flora's song quite a bit, adding the new lines and verses as she made them up.

It would actually be pretty good once it was finished and polished. I could hear exactly how it should sound in my head, but I didn't try singing myself yet.

I was too afraid to use my voice, worried that I might wreck it or mess up the healing process, but I hummed all the time, and I knew that there would be a time, not too long in the future, that I would start singing again.

One sunny afternoon after chores were done and I was dreamily sitting at my window watching the horses in the pasture, I finally got the phone call I'd been waiting for. The one from my mom, but it didn't go quite as planned.

"Adie," she said, sounding frantic. "I'm so sorry to tell you this. Grady has run away. We have no idea where he is."

"You let him run away?" I could not keep the anger out of my voice.

"Of course we didn't *let* him run away. He left last night while we were out. He was supposed to be babysitting. He left the little kids all alone. I can't believe he'd be this irresponsible."

"Are you serious? Have you not gotten any of my messages? He's been miserable. Flora said Phil hit him."

There was a long silence, and I heard my mom sniffling.

"Yes, yes I did. I'm sorry, we've been so busy that I didn't call you back right away. But I think Flora must have exaggerated. They just got into an argument, that's all, and Grady fell. Phil said—"

"Phil is a grown man and Grady is thirteen years old," I said flatly. "There is no excuse for that."

"No, you're right. There isn't. Everyone is under a lot of pressure right now. You wouldn't believe the hours we're putting in. It's more exhausting than I'd expected."

I was too angry to answer.

"Anyway, I wanted to tell you about Grady. We're just frantic. He doesn't know the city at all. I hoped he might have told you where he was going. He didn't leave a note. He didn't say anything to us. The police are looking for him, of course."

My thoughts spun wildly, making a rapid list of all the places Grady might have snuck off to. Were there any comic conventions coming up that he'd talked about with me before I'd left? Any concerts? I knew he missed his friends back home most of all.

"The old farm," I said finally, "he's probably going there."

"Oh dear, we're in New York state right now. The farm is

thousands of miles away. Do you think so? Is that something he would actually do?" She sounded completely lost and bewildered.

You would know that if you took even a second to talk to him and figure out what type of person he is, I thought.

"Yes. That is exactly what he'd do. Look, I can't talk right now. I'm honestly too mad at you to have this conversation right now. I'm hanging up. Call me the second you hear anything."

"Adie, I'm—"

But I hung up before she could say anything else. I was much too angry to keep listening to her. What was the point of having eight children at all if you were too busy to spend any time with them? Or not help them when they were miserable or keep your abusive manager from tormenting them? Seriously, what kind of parent did that?

My brother is missing, I thought numbly, *he doesn't have a cell phone or any money and he's in a strange city. And I'm stuck here, and I don't even begin to know how to help him.*

Everyone was sympathetic that afternoon when I told them what had happened.

But there was no question of me going to look for him.

"The police will find him, I'm sure," Julie said with a confidence that I didn't think either of us felt. "Besides, what if he tries to come here to find you? You should definitely stay put until we know more. You won't be able to do much good if you go back anyway."

She was right. They definitely didn't need me getting in the way. And I would probably kill Phil if I saw him right then, even the thought of him made my blood boil. It wasn't like I knew the neighbourhood and would be any help with searching. And there was a tiny possibility that Grady might be trying to actually make it here instead of our old farm.

For the short term, it was better if I stayed put.

· · ·

For the next week, I just tried to keep myself as busy as possible. My mom called every single day and, now that they'd put their tour on hold, I was able to speak to my dad, Micah, and Mariam more often, too. But there was never any news about Grady. It was like he'd just disappeared into thin air.

What if Phil has done something to him? I thought in desperation one day, but I pushed the thought determinedly away. Phil was gross and mean but he wasn't a kidnapper. He wasn't a murderer. No, Grady had to be out there somewhere.

CHAPTER 20

BREE

"Hey, I've been doing some thinking about Adie," Julie said slowly, tossing another forkful of soiled bedding into the wheelbarrow. "I want to do something nice for her."

I stopped sweeping the aisle and looked up, "Me too. That's horrible about her brother. What sort of thing were you thinking about?"

"Well, I wonder if doing some more riding lessons might help her take her mind off things. She works so hard but then she spends all the rest of her time cooped up in her room, worrying. She needs a distraction. Something fun."

"She takes Bear out almost every day," I reminded her.

"But that's just for like twenty minutes. I wanted to give her a goal to focus on."

"Okay, so what were you thinking?"

"I guess I'm asking if you'd let her ride Ace. Not all the time, but a few days a week. I'll give her lessons. Maybe we could plan for a show this summer. She could take him in a few classes."

"But Ace is a baby," I protested. "he's not ready."

"Yeah, but he's the world's oldest baby. He has the soul of a much more mature horse. I have yet to see him look wrong at anything let alone spook. And she'd be happy just paddling around on him on a loose rein. I think it would mean the world to her."

For a second, I felt a tug of jealousy, a nasty little jolt in my heart and stomach that made me feel a bit ill. Ace was *my* horse, after all. And then I pushed it resolutely away. Adie was my friend, and she was hurting. Ace would be perfect.

"Of course she can," I said finally. "Yes, absolutely."

"Thanks Bree, that's great. I think that would really mean a lot to Adie."

I thought of how lucky I'd been for Lorne to bring me here in the first place. He'd loaned me Bear so I could first learn to ride, and Julie let me ride Nipper all the time. That must not have been easy for her, especially when I'd been an uncoordinated beginner. This was the least I could do to return the favour.

I felt much better that night when I saw Adie's face light up with delight when Julie told her she'd be riding Ace the next day. It was like watching a kid on Christmas morning.

"Oh, thank you, Bree," she said turning to me right away. "As long as you're sure."

"Of course I'm sure," I said, and meant it.

The next morning, I kept half an eye on her as I tacked up Nipper. There were still dark hollows around her eyes from all the sleepless nights she'd had lately, but she looked so happy quietly grooming Ace. She brushed him carefully and settled his tack onto him like he was about to go into the show ring.

Ace took the change in handlers in his usual good stride and calmly walked toward the mounting block without looking back at me.

It was like watching a little kid go off to school without you on the first day of class.

"Ow, Nipper what was that for?" I said, rubbing my wrist where his sharp teeth had grabbed me. He hadn't done that to me in a long time, not since I'd first started riding him. "What, are you jealous?"

He practically dragged me to the mounting block, and I forced myself to not let my thoughts wander to Ace so much. It was dangerous not to focus fully on what I was doing. Lorne had taught me that right from the beginning. Horses lived in the now, not the past or the future and, if you wanted to be safe as a rider, you had to stay in the now, too.

As if agreeing with me, Nipper let out a big snort and gave himself a shake from head to tail like a dog after a bath. He didn't try and bite again as I let down his stirrups, checked his girth, and then climbed aboard. He stood rock-still with his ears pricked. And it was like he made an extra effort to be perfectly obedient for the entire ride.

And actually, it was fun to have a lesson with someone else in the ring. Julie focused mostly on Adie since she needed the extra help, but she would turn now and then and give me instructions and corrections, too.

Surprisingly, it wasn't hard at all to see Ace being ridden by someone else. Adie looked like she was glowing from the inside, she was so happy, and she took every bit of advice Julie gave her.

I had to admit that she looked much better on Ace than she did on Nipper. After the first walk circle, you could see her whole body relax and then the smile never left her face.

She also seemed happy to let Ace saunter along at a snail's pace, something that would have driven me crazy if I had been on board. I was always encouraging Ace to go forward, for his strides to be more like Nipper's smooth, elastic paces.

I had to admit that he looked pretty happy and relaxed to be toddling along at his own speed.

I was in such a good mood when I headed back up to the house to change that the unexpected phone call completely caught me off guard.

That's Dr.Grace's office, I thought, my heart thundering in my chest as I looked at the number flashing on my phone. My appointment wasn't scheduled for another few weeks. Why would they be calling?

"Hello, Bree speaking," I said, trying to keep my voice steady.

You're fine, the results are going to come back fine, I told myself firmly.

"Hi there, this is Brenda from Dr. Grace's office."

"Hello," I said cautiously. This was a new receptionist I hadn't met before.

"Dr. Grace wanted me to let you know that there was a big issue with your bloodwork, and she wants you to bump up your appointment date. Can you come this week instead?"

My heart fell and I reached out to steady myself on the desk by the window.

"Um, sure," I managed, "whenever you like. What kind of problem?"

"Oh, sorry, I really have no idea. I'm kind of new here. I'm just passing on what she said. She told me that we should make an appointment as soon as possible. Does Friday at ten o'clock work for you?"

"I guess so," I said. My voice came out a squeak. I felt cold and numb. I could hardly believe this was happening. It must be awful news if she wanted me to come in early so she could give me the results in person.

"Great!" the receptionist said in a way too chipper voice. "See you then. Have a fantastic day."

And the line went dead.

Tears stung my eyes and my breath came in short gasps. I stumbled to the bed and sat down hard.

How could I be sick again when I felt perfectly fine? It wasn't fair. I had been healthy for so long. I'd gotten my wish to ride horses, to work on a farm, and to get healthy again. So many miraculous things had happened to me in the last seven months. But I wasn't ready to stop now. It didn't make sense that everything would all be taken away from me again. At least not so soon.

The phone rang again in my hand, startling me so bad that I almost dropped it.

Nicholas. I stared down at the screen, hesitated, and then just let it go to voicemail.

You're a coward, I thought, *Nicholas is your friend.* But I couldn't face talking to him now. I couldn't hear all about how wonderful his life at school was when my own life might be circling down the drain yet again.

It would be better if he just forgot about me completely.

CHAPTER 21

BREE

I wasn't sure how long I sat there in my bed just staring at the wall. I'm pretty sure I was in shock. But gradually, I felt the bed underneath me, and heard the birds singing outside. I remembered that I was only half-changed out of my breeches and that I was cold and tired after my ride. And hungry.

I took a deep breath and felt my numb limbs come back to life.

Right, so that was awful, I told myself, *but I'm not dead yet, no matter what happens at that appointment on Friday. I need to pull myself together. I'm going to enjoy every last minute I have on this earth.*

The first step was heading downstairs for tea and a snack. I was lucky that the kitchen was empty. I wasn't ready to talk to anyone quite yet. Funnily enough, what I really wanted to do was write.

It had nothing to do with the subject of the shocking phone call, either.

Watching Adie transform on Ace earlier had really got me thinking. She had looked like a much different rider than she had on Nipper. It had really been like night and day. How much did finding the right horse and human partnership influence becoming a good rider?

Finding the Right Dance Partner, I typed, and I didn't stop writing until the sky outside had darkened and Julie had called me three times to come down for dinner.

"What were you working on?" she asked when I finally came downstairs.

I blinked at the light and noise in the kitchen, disoriented for a second. Sometimes when I really got caught up in writing, it was like I completely disappeared into a different world and forgot about who or where I was. Coming back to reality was a little bit of an adjustment.

The whole kitchen was full. Chloe had a week off from school for break and she'd decided to stay over a few nights. Jeremy was there, although he didn't always come up to the house to eat, and so was Lorne and Adie.

"Um, it's about how different people and different horses mesh," I said, taking my plate to the stove and piling on a heap of pasta. "I thought it would help in matching up the thoroughbreds with their new owners."

"Oh definitely, that's a big consideration," Julie said approvingly. "We have to match the rider's skill levels and goals, but also make sure the match is the right mix of personalities, too. And it's not always easy to know what type of horse you get along with and like to ride until you've had lots of experience with different types. It's one of those things that you can't know until you know."

Like riding Ace, I thought guiltily. *Even though I love him best, Nipper is actually more my type under saddle.*

"And the type of horse you like can change, too," Chloe piped up. "I used to hate hot, forward horses when I was starting out and now that's the only type of horse I really enjoy riding."

"Gretta loved spicy horses," Lorne said fondly, "but as she got older, she realized that they had to have a really level brain, too. There's no point in having a lot of forward energy in a horse that is too anxious to control. Or who is too willful to partner up with you. There is a balance."

"And horses change, too," Jeremy added, "today's hot four-year-old might be tomorrow's dead quiet eight-year-old. Or a two-year-old slug might become hotter and more interesting once they learn to love going forward."

"Like Ace," Julie said, looking at me meaningfully.

"What about Ace? He's already perfect," Adie said around a mouthful of pasta and I had to laugh.

"Knowing which horses you get along with best just makes good business sense, too," Lorne was saying, still caught up on the subject.

"When we were first starting out, Gretta and I just rode anything we could get our hands on. We couldn't afford to be choosy, so we rode them all.

"But as we got more experienced, we learned which types of horses would be easiest for us to get along with. Animals we could quickly produce into the type of athletes we needed without much fuss. Hot horses became our go-to because they were already eager to go and you didn't have to spend half your time waking them up and convincing them that going forward was fun.

"We left the slower, safer horses for people who appreciated them. And we took on hotter, bolder, and maybe more badly behaved horses, from people who couldn't handle them. It was a good system for us."

I listened to them discuss it while I ate, filing it all away to add the more interesting bits to my blog later. I couldn't wait until summer when we could start meeting the new potential adopters for our horses.

It would be so rewarding to place them in new homes where they could flourish.

We'd made the decision early on not to adopt out the horses while they were still green and inexperienced. We wanted our October Horses graduates to not only have a solid education under saddle, but also to have some experience at shows, trail riding, and other excursions so we could pass them on to their new homes with confidence.

I wonder if I'll even make it to summer, I thought suddenly, then pushed the idea roughly away. I was *definitely* going to make it until summer. Even if I had to go back into treatment, I would make it that far no matter what.

CHAPTER 22

BREE

*T*he next few days were bright and sunny, and we took full advantage of that to ride whenever we could.

Now that I was desperate to have as many precious hours in the saddle as possible, I almost regretted loaning Ace to Adie. I rode Nipper every day and took out Ace on the days that Adie rode Bear. But, with all that nervous energy to burn off in the days leading up to my appointment, I could have easily ridden one or even two more horses a day.

Jeremy had been conditioning Timely and Rabbit daily. He only took them in the ring a couple days a week and all his other rides were about building up their strength and endurance out on the trails.

With Lorne's approval, he had put his two horses into a program of progressively longer conditioning rides over various types of terrain. He was a big believer in hill work, and he and Chloe would spend hours out with the horses in the big fields behind the farm.

Chloe had protested against riding with him at first, but Lorne had insisted that it was safer and more productive if they exercised the horses together.

They'd even set up a low course of logs and poles that they could play around with. And Chloe had been in her element sailing over them with Dragon and Nugget.

Timely was coming along nicely, but Jeremy had refused to jump Rabbit over more than a few ground-poles.

"It's not worth my neck," he'd said, shrugging when Lorne questioned him. "Look at the way he hangs his knees."

"Well, you can't expect him to round-up over a pole on the ground," Chloe had argued. "He needs something to challenge him. A good trainer could develop his talent, not give up on him."

"I've seen a lot of horses in my time, miss," Jeremy told her, "I know when I meet one that needs to keep all four legs on the ground. You're welcome to hop on and give him a go if you like. But don't ask me to drive you to the hospital afterward."

"Well, maybe you'll change your mind once he's further along," Lorne had said mildly, but Jeremy had merely shaken his head knowingly.

The horses liked Jeremy, and even Chloe grudgingly admitted that he was all right in the saddle, even if he was *old*.

He wasn't overly affectionate with the horses; he didn't fuss over them at all. But he had light hands and a good seat. He was fair to them and always made sure they were taken care of properly.

"I still don't trust him, though," Chloe told me nearly every day, "there is something shifty about him. I might see if I can live here for the summer after all. Somebody needs to keep a close eye on him."

I really hoped that she would be allowed to come stay with us, even just for the summer. It had become increasingly obvious that she was struggling to get out to the farm to ride as often as she wanted. Her exams were coming up fast and her mother always complained that she needed her to help out more at home. Adding Nugget to her workload had made it painfully obvious how overwhelmed she was.

As much as Chloe disliked him, having Jeremy around to help with stalls and to do handiwork around the farm was a big relief to me. He was a hard worker when he put his mind to it. And if he was given a list of chores to do, he would just power through them until he was done, hardly taking any breaks at all.

Still, as much as Jeremy had made himself fit in with the farm, and as much as Lorne liked him, there was something that never quite sat right with me about him.

Chloe was sure that she would catch him drinking on the job or smoking or doing drugs, but he never did anything like that around the horses. He always appeared at the barn first thing in the morning ready to work.

But late at night Lorne's car would creep out of the driveway and sometimes it wouldn't come back until two or three in the morning.

I never knew where he was going, and Lorne was adamant that we not bother him about it.

"He's a grown man," Lorne insisted. "And if he asks me to borrow the car from time to time so he can go out and blow off steam, then who am I to deny him? He does his work and that's all we can ask."

Still, I agreed with Chloe that we should keep a close eye on him.

CHAPTER 23

BREE

The day of my terrifying appointment finally arrived. I woke up with a lump of fear in my throat and my palms already sweaty with fear.

I did my chores as usual, determined not to let this day rob me of even a single second I spent with the horses. I didn't ride, though. I was saving that for the afternoon. I needed something good to look forward to.

"Are you positive you don't want anyone to go with you?" Julie asked, doing her best to sound nonchalant. But I could hear the tremor in her voice. "I can come. Or we could call your dad. Or you could call Nicholas … I'm sure he'd like to—"

"No," I said quickly. "I don't want to bother anyone. Especially not Nicholas. It's no big deal. Really."

All lies. All I wanted to do was lean on someone's shoulder and cry and have them make it all better. But that wasn't going to happen.

It was better if I went and faced it on my own. And, if it really was bad news, I wanted time to process it by myself before I had to tell anyone. Especially Nicholas.

"Well, drive safely then," Julie said reluctantly, clearly not happy with my decision. "And call me if you need anything. Even if you just want to talk while you're waiting."

"Thanks, I will," I said, grabbing the keys to Lorne's car and a jacket before she could say anything else.

It was one of those fresh spring days where the air smelled sweet, and you could feel summer just around the corner. It was completely at odds with my current state of terror.

To cheer myself up, I rolled the window down and let the fresh breeze blow in across my hair. So what if it got messed up. Who knew how many days I had left to enjoy the spring time?

Dr. Grace's office was a few blocks from the hospital downtown. It took me a few minutes to find a parking spot but even then, I was still too early. I busied myself scrolling through my phone looking at photos of the horses to try and calm down.

The phone buzzed in my hands and I jerked back as Nicholas' name and photo appeared on my screen.

No, I can't talk to him now, I thought, declining his call. *I'll talk to him tonight. I'll call him afterwards and catch him up on everything that's been going on.*

I looked at the clock and closed my eyes for a second, not wanting to leave the car.

You can do this, I told myself firmly, forcing my reluctant feet out of the car, down the sidewalk, and up the long ramp that led to the building.

Inside, there was an elevator that led upstairs, but I was too jittery to use it. I felt like I needed to keep moving to keep my panic at bay.

Upstairs, I pushed through the glass doors and wiped my sweating palms on my jeans.

"Hi there," a beaming young receptionist said, standing up behind her desk. I'd never seen her before so I assumed she was the new receptionist I'd talked to on the phone. "You must be Breanna. Have a seat and Dr. Grace will be with you soon."

"Okay," I said with a sigh, sliding into a plush red chair to the left of the door. I picked up my phone again and started scrolling through my photos, but I wasn't even seeing them this time. I felt sick to my stomach and I couldn't make my heart stop pounding. I felt like I was going to pass out.

I'd pretty much worked my way to the edge of tears by the time Dr. Grace appeared in the hallway, beckoning toward her office with a wide smile.

Her smile faded away as she saw the expression on my face, and she looked even more concerned when I promptly burst into tears the second the office door was closed.

"Bree," she said in astonishment, laying a sympathetic hand on my shoulder. "What on earth is the matter? Don't you feel well?"

"It's come back, hasn't it?" I said, putting one hand over my eyes to block out the room, the specialist, and the situation as if by keeping them closed I could put off reality forever. "Just tell me. How long do I have?"

"How long—? Oh, no, no, no. Bree, there is nothing wrong with your results. Didn't the receptionist say why I wanted to see you so soon?

"The lab forgot to pull an extra sample for one of the research studies and it's pretty time sensitive. There is some paperwork they need you to fill out. I just figured I'd go over the results in detail with you when you got here and get that last sample. Didn't Brenda tell you all this on the phone?"

"N-no," I stuttered, hardly believing that I could be hearing her right. "She said there was an issue with the bloodwork. I thought—"

"Oh dear, I'm so sorry. You must have been frantic with worry. No, sweetie, everything is looking fantastic. You're still feeling good, right? I mean, apart from today?"

"Yes, I'm great. I mean, I had a hard winter, but I feel so much better now that the cold is gone. I just thought—" I took a deep breath and pulled myself together with difficulty. I knew if I didn't get a handle on myself that I'd start sobbing again and not stop for a week.

"Here, sit down. There is a box of tissues on the desk. We'll go over your results right now and get that paperwork signed. The doctors who are running the study you're part of are so excited with your results, Bree. You're one of a few really nice success stories, and they think that this medication is going to help a lot of people get a second chance at life."

"That's great," I said. And I meant it, I was glad for those other people who'd had miraculous recoveries just like me. But right then, I was only thinking of myself. And how I was going to actually walk out of here with a real future.

I tried to pay close attention to Dr. Grace as she laid out the lab sheets in front of me and pointed her way down the graph, carefully explaining what each result meant. But now that I knew I was going to live, I just wanted to run outside into the sunshine and dance and shout and then go home and ride some horses.

"I'll print these off for you, of course, so you have a copy for your own records. We'll just pull the blood here, if that's okay, and then the nurse will run it over to the lab next door."

I found myself nodding and following her to the nurse's station where they expertly, painlessly, found a vein and pulled a vial of my blood. In a daze, I signed the papers for the next phase of the drug study and finally made my way back to the waiting room.

"There's a gentleman here for you," Brenda, the world's worst receptionist said, beaming at me, totally ignorant of the emotional hell she'd put me through.

I was still in a dreamy haze when I looked up and saw Nicholas sitting on one of the red, plush chairs. He had a magazine nervously rolled between his hands and his expression was tense.

"Bree." He stood up and came toward me, taking one of my hands and staring down worriedly at my face. It was probably still blotchy and red from crying.

"It's okay," I said, feeling tears well up all over again. But this time they were happy tears. "It was a mistake. I'm fine. I'm going to be fine for at least a while."

"Oh, thank god." And before I could say anything else, he was crushing me tightly against his chest and I could hear his heartbeat pounding away as if he'd just run a marathon.

Instead of pulling away, I leaned right against him and let him hold me up. Letting his solid strength and warmth soak into me.

"I'm glad you're here. How did you know to come?" I murmured against his shirt.

"I don't know. I just had a feeling that something wasn't right. I couldn't get ahold of you, so I called my mom. She told me where to find you. Bree I—" He pushed me back so he could look into my face again. "You know that I couldn't stand if anything was to happen to you, right?"

I nodded and wiped my eyes. "I know, that's why I didn't want to bother you."

"Crazy girl," he said. "Silly girl. Don't you know—" He took a deep breath. "Come on, we're going out to lunch to celebrate."

All I had been thinking of was getting home as fast as I could to see the horses. But, yes, my good news really did deserve a celebration.

"I'll make a deal with you," I said. "I'll come to lunch if you agree to go trail riding with me this weekend."

"Ugh," he said, laughing and wrinkling his nose, "like on a horse?"

"Yes, definitely on a horse. Is it a deal?"

"Deal," he said. He reached out to catch my hand but instead of stopping with that he pulled me toward him again and leaned over so his mouth was firmly pressed against mine, sending shock waves of surprised happiness through me.

"Well," the receptionist said, sounding a little scandalized, "best to take that outside, kids. You two have a fantastic day now."

"Oh, we will, Brenda," I said as we broke apart, both of us laughing like little kids.

And, linking hands, we got out of there as fast as we could.

CHAPTER 24

BREE

*B*ut the surprises didn't end completely that day. I got home late in the afternoon, after a long lunch at a fancy, upscale restaurant, where we spent a few hours catching up and sharing dessert.

Nicholas even got the waiter to bring us some glasses of wine so we could toast to my recovery. Something that felt incredibly grown up and wonderful even though I only drank a few sips of mine.

Nicholas had to go back to school afterward, he'd missed classes to meet me, but he promised to come home Friday afternoon and stay for a few days.

I'd planned on taking Nipper for a celebratory canter on the trails the second I got home but life, like usual, had other plans. Instead of a trail ride, I got a strange, cryptic phone call from Angelika.

"I'm on the ferry headed your way," she said in a stage whisper, not bothering to start with something *normal* like hello. "I just wanted to make sure you were home."

"I'm home. Why are you driving here? You normally fly in."

"Er, yes. Well, I just needed to drive this time. So you'll be home all day? Is Adeline there?"

"She's here," I said, looking over to where Adie was sitting at the kitchen table cleaning a bridle. She'd pulled it all apart and had the pieces spread out in front of her. But she had a far off look on her face and didn't look like she was even paying attention to what she was doing. She just moved the damp, soapy cloth across the same bit of leather over and over.

"Right, I'll be there in about an hour then. Just don't go anywhere, okay? Promise me. This is important."

"Where would I go?" I started to ask but she'd already hung up. Typical Angelika. Always the drama queen.

"That was Angelika," I told Adie, "she's on her way."

"She is?" Adie said, coming out of her daze with a shake of her head. "I thought she was still on her tour."

"I have no idea." I shrugged. "But she says she's coming for a visit."

"Well, it will be nice to see her," Adie said, looking back down at the bridle and picking up another piece of leather. "I really do need to thank her for sending me here. Besides Grady going missing, this has been great."

"We love having you here. And I'm glad you're enjoying Ace so much."

"He's definitely the best thing that's happened to me in a long time," Adie said. She smiled at me, but I could see how much of a strain her brother's disappearance had put on her.

I hoped, for everyone's sake, that he would be found safely soon.

CHAPTER 25

ADIE

I was doing a terrible job putting Bear's bridle back together, almost as bad a job as I had done cleaning it. I just couldn't seem to concentrate, and now I couldn't make the pieces go back together properly again.

I had just stood up to stretch out my cramped muscles when a strange car pulled up to the house.

It was a shiny burgundy rental car with American plates, and I stood up on tiptoes so I could see better. The car windows were tinted so I couldn't see inside, but I assumed that it was Angelika.

"Hey, Bree, your sister is here," I called over my shoulder to where she was in the living room, sitting cross-legged on the couch, working on her laptop.

"Fantastic," she said in an unenthusiastic voice.

I went to put my empty tea-mug in the sink, half-glancing out the window again toward the car. Suddenly, I froze, my whole body going numb with shock. The cup slipped through my fingers and landed in the sink with a sharp cracking sound.

"Grady!" I screamed and was running down the hall and out the front door so fast that I didn't even stop to put shoes on. I ran down the steps, crashing into my bewildered looking brother full-force and wrapping him in a tight hug.

"You're alive. You're alive. You're alive," I said over and over hysterically, not able to stop myself. "You're really okay."

"Of course I'm okay, let go, you're choking me."

I stepped back to look at him and some of my fear shifted into anger. He didn't look injured; he didn't look starving or traumatized. He'd cut his long hair short, but other than that he was the same old Grady.

"Where were you? Do you know how worried we all were? We thought you'd been killed. Or worse. How could you run away and not tell anyone where you were going? We were so scared. I was—" I began to cry, my whole body shaking with adrenaline.

"Okay, okay. I'm sorry. Really, Adie, I mean it. I'm sorry. I didn't mean to scare you. I just needed to get away and figure some things out. I'm fine."

"But, how did you survive out there?" I said between sniffles. "You didn't have any money. And how did you meet up with Angelika? Why didn't you call?"

"I didn't have a phone to use, at first. And I sold my guitar at a pawn shop before I left. And, well, I stole some money from Hope."

"Oh, my gosh, Grady, you didn't."

"I did. And I'm not sorry about that. She was keeping it for herself anyway and not sharing with the rest of us. I hopped on a bus so I could find Angelika. It was no big deal. Nobody stopped me or anything. I thought maybe she could help me like she'd helped you."

"Oh, Grady." I hugged him again and wiped away the tears that just wouldn't stop falling. "Don't ever do something like that again."

"Hey, do you think we could go inside?" Angelika asked. "I've been driving for days."

"Of course, I'm sorry. Come in. And thank you so much for taking care of him. Thanks for everything."

Bree stood up with astonishment when we came in and listened open-mouthed as I quickly explained the situation to her.

"But why didn't you take him back to his parents?" she asked her sister in astonishment.

"I asked, well, I kind of begged, her not to," Grady said. "I told her I would have just run away again before we got there anyway. I thought about taking the bus back to our old farm, but I was afraid I'd get stopped at the border. They'd think a kid on their own was suspicious."

"Well, you're lucky they let you through in the car," Bree said, "didn't they check your passports?"

"Yes," Angelika said, "I mean they glanced at them but they didn't ask questions or anything. I did have to give my autograph to a few officers who recognized me, though."

"Of course you did." Bree rolled her eyes, but a smile tugged at her mouth. "You could have gotten into a lot of trouble, though. They might have thought you'd kidnapped him."

"Well, I didn't steal him and we didn't get in trouble. Grady could have just explained everything to them if we'd been caught. It was no big deal. You guys owe me big time for this. I hope you know I'm staying for the weekend so I can catch up on sleep. And I want a horse ride out of this. Bree can put a picture of me riding on her blog. I'll be a hero."

"We need to call Mom," I told Grady firmly. "Everyone has been frantic."

"I know. We will. But I want to talk to you first. I have some things to tell you."

"Sure, we can talk all you like. But I'm calling mom right now." I pulled out my phone and went to hit her number.

"Wait," Grady said, reaching out to grab my wrist. "Adie. You're not listening. I need to talk to you first. It was Hope."

"What do you mean? That she was keeping money for herself?"

"No. Adie, Hope started the fire. She's the one who nearly burned our house down. She almost killed us."

We just stared at each other in silence. And then I sat down hard on the couch. My legs suddenly couldn't support my weight anymore.

"Um, we'll just let you guys talk," Angelika said, "Come help me in the kitchen, Bree. I could really use a snack."

After that, we sat on the couch talking for a long, long time.

"I tried to tell you that night," Grady said, "but afterwards, for a long time, I half-thought I must have imagined it."

Grady had seen Hope crouching down doing something in the stairwell that night of the fire. He'd been on his way to sneak outside to go for a midnight walk in the way he did sometimes when he couldn't sleep. But when he'd reached the stairs, he'd seen Hope crouching there in the half-darkness. She'd had something small and shiny in her hands and she was doing something to the power outlet that was located halfway up the stairs.

"She had the weirdest look on her face," he said, shuddering a little. "I almost didn't recognize her. It creeped me out so I just went back to my room before she could see me. The next thing I knew, you and Flora came to get me and said there was a fire.

"Afterwards, when they said that the fire had started in our stairwell, I was sure she'd had something to do with it. I thought she might confess or say something, but she never did. She just acted like the fire had nothing to do with her at all.

"After a while, I wondered if I'd just imagined the whole thing. It wasn't until later that I was really sure."

"I can't believe this," I said, looking down at my hands in my lap. "I mean, I know Hope thought there were too many of us sometimes, that mom should have stopped having kids after

Mariam was born. And I knew she was jealous that she didn't get enough attention. But I never thought—"

"I don't think it was us, Adie. I don't think she meant to hurt anyone on purpose. I think she just hated being stuck on the farm and didn't know how else to get away. And I guess it worked because that's what convinced Dad to finally move."

"I'm sorry, Grady. I wish you'd come to me about this a long time ago. Why did you speak up now, though?"

"Because of Phil. I overheard them fighting over it one night in his hotel room and he caught me listening. That's when he hit me. He'd known about it all along. He probably pushed her to do it."

"Seriously?"

"Well, I don't have any proof of that. But probably. He's that type of guy."

Yes, he is, I thought. *And Hope is that type of girl.*

I should have been filled with anger, but all I felt right then was sadness. She could have killed us all. And despite what Grady had said, I didn't think she would have actually minded if we had all conveniently disappeared that night.

After that revelation, I made Grady sit beside me while I made the dreaded phone call to Mom.

I really didn't know how I was going to say any of this to her, but my family at least needed to know that Grady was safe. They'd been worried sick. Most of them anyway.

At first, she just cried and cried when I told her that Grady had been found alive and well. And I could hear Dad's voice and Mariam's voice in the background clamouring with questions next to the phone.

"I'll be on the first plane there," she'd said between sobs. "We all will. I'll book it right now. I don't care about the cost."

"No, Mom, wait," I'd said, "don't do anything yet. Grady has something to tell you and you need to listen carefully, okay?"

I made sure she was actually listening before I handed Grady the phone.

And I held my brother's hand while his words pulled our family completely apart.

CHAPTER 26

BREE

$\mathcal{A}$die and her brother talked for a long time while Angelika and I tried not to eavesdrop from the kitchen.

I went over and put on a fresh pot of coffee while Angelika pulled out a chair from the table and sank wearily into it.

"You should have taken him to his parents," I told her again. "You could have gotten into serious trouble. The police are looking all over for him."

"Maybe," she said, yawning. "But that's not what he wanted. When he told me the whole story, I just agreed to bring him here. It seemed like the simplest choice."

It didn't seem simple at all to me but I let it go.

The coffee maker began to chug away purposefully and I filled a plate with cookies and set it down in front of my sister.

"Thanks," she said, sending me a tired smile. "And thanks again for taking Adie in. I'm so glad that worked out."

"She's fantastic," I agreed. "But I still don't understand why you sent her here in the first place. I mean, she was a stranger to you. And when you asked if she could come stay with us you acted like you knew her really well."

"Did I?" Angelika said innocently, opening her eyes wide. That was the exact look she always used when she was trying to weasel out of trouble.

"Um, yeah, you did. And it turns out that you'd met her like once. Don't get me wrong, we love having her here. It just seems strange that you put yourself out for a stranger."

A flash of irritation crossed Angelika's face and then she sighed again and picked up a cookie.

"Fine. Yes, I'd only met their family a few times. But everyone knows them. And it was obvious that their creepy manager was hard on those kids, especially Adie. Anyone but their parents could see that. The music scene here isn't huge so you end up knowing everything about everyone eventually.

"I caught him yelling at Adie, saying awful things, and I could just tell by the look on her face that her life was about to head on a downward spiral. It's so easy for young performers to get lost in that world. So, I stepped in."

"Oh," I said, filling our mugs and bringing them to the table. "That was really nice of you."

"Yeah, probably. But people did the same thing for me when I was young and knew nothing. I made some mistakes with drinking and drugs and it was having people there in my corner that turned me around. I wanted to help Adie before she felt desperate enough to travel down that road.

I looked up guiltily, a hot flush stinging my cheeks. I hadn't had much to do with Angelika back when she'd hit her rough patch. I'd been angry at her still and hadn't cared about what had been happening in her life at the time. I hadn't been one of those people in her corner at all.

"I'm sorry that I was such a terrible sister while we growing up," I said suddenly, "I really wasn't there for you and that was wrong. And I apologize."

She stared at me, stunned, the coffee cup pressed tightly between her palms.

"Well, I was a pretty awful younger sister, too," she said finally, clearing her throat.

"No, but I was the older one. I should have been the one looking out for you. It was my fault, not yours."

She blinked a few times, her eyes welling up just a little before she wiped any traces of tears away impatiently.

"How about we just settle on blaming mom and dad for everything? That's probably easiest. They're pretty crazy."

I burst out laughing and so did she. I reached out to squeeze her hand and she clutched mine tightly for a second before letting go.

When Julie and Lorne came back to the house, we ushered them into the kitchen to explain about Grady as best we could.

When Adie came back into the kitchen, she looked exhausted but happy, too.

"Would you be okay if Grady stayed for a few more days?" she asked Julie. "It's going to take our parents a while to sort things out. Things are a little complicated over there. Only if it's okay, though."

"Of course it is," Julie had said, beaming at Grady. "You remind me of my son Nicholas when he was your age. Do you need a lunch or a shower or a rest after your long trip?"

"Um, I'm kind of hungry," Grady said, eyeing up our half-eaten plate of cookies. "And then do you think I could see the horses?"

"I think that could be arranged," Julie said, beaming at him.

The whole weekend seemed like one long celebration after that.

Everyone was just so relieved that Grady had been found

alive. And once the excitement of *that* had died down a little, I shared my own good news.

Instead of having a nap that afternoon like she'd threatened to, Angelika let me loan her a pair of breeches and my helmet and we went down to the ring and brought out Bear and Ace.

Julie gave both Grady and Angelika a little horsemanship lesson and then let them climb aboard and toddle around the ring.

"I can't believe I'm actually riding Ace," Angelika said, her face lit up with happiness. "Do you think we can go over a jump now?"

"Um, maybe next year," Julie said, laughing, "let's work on some steering for now."

I was shocked at how excited Angelika was to be riding. She kept a huge smile on her face the whole time and was constantly petting Ace and telling him he was a superstar.

"Maybe, one of Eddie's horses will be ready for you to ride by the end of the summer," I told her. "We could plan for a trail ride."

"Or I could gallop on the beach," she said dreamily, "you could take pictures of me riding in a long dress with bare feet and the wind blowing through my hair. That would look amazing."

Or, maybe not at all, I thought, keeping a smile on my face with effort.

She did get her wish to have her photo in my next blog, though. We ended up with a great picture of her posing on Ace with Adie standing on the ground beside her.

They looked so alike that they could have been sisters. And their huge smiles completely matched, too.

It had definitely been the type of day where everyone's dreams had come true.

CHAPTER 27

ADIE

"*H*ey, Adie, do you mind if I interrupt you?"

I looked up to see Julie standing in the doorway to the living room where we'd been practicing, a shy smile on her face.

"Of course, come in, we're just fooling around with this song. We wanted to get it ready for Flora before she gets here this afternoon. She's going to be so excited that Angelika is helping with it."

Flora had been through so much in the last year, we all had, but Grady and I had wanted to do something special just for her.

"Well, I just wondered if you could use this? I heard that Grady had to sell his guitar. I thought maybe this would help with your song."

She held out the black guitar toward us lovingly, like it was a child, and I knew that somehow it was special to her.

"Oh, wow, thank you," I said, setting my pen and paper aside. I slid down on the couch so I could make room for her to sit down.

"It was my husband's," she said slowly. "He loved to play. He and his friends even had a band. Nothing serious. They were just having fun, but I loved to listen to them. He had the most beautiful voice."

I nodded, not knowing what to say. I knew that her husband, Nicholas's dad, had died in the same car crash that had caused all the burns on her body. She had lost way more in her accident than I had in mine.

"I was going to hand it down to Nicholas someday, but he really isn't the musical type. I would love to lend it to you while you're here, if you like. Even if you can't sing yet, I think you should have something to play."

"Oh, thank you," I said, reaching over impulsively and giving her a hug.

"It's been sitting a long time," she says shyly. "I'm not sure if it will even sound right anymore. I don't know anything about music, but it might need to be tuned or something."

I cradled it in my lap, touching the strings with my fingers, tightening and loosening and adjusting. I plucked a string and listened to the hollow reverberations that moved through the wooden body and then through me, like I was the one being tuned.

The smile on my face was completely involuntary.

"Does it sound okay?" Julie asked anxiously. "Is it still usable?"

"Yeah," I said, trying to tamp down my excitement. "Yeah, it's fine. I can tune it for you and clean it up. Thanks, Julie."

"Oh, I'm so glad you like it. Well, I'll leave you kids alone to practice. You just call if you need anything."

I sat cross-legged on the couch and plucked another string, holding my hand flat against the wood so I could feel the vibrations. They were like an old, beloved language that I'd tried, briefly, to forget.

No matter what happened to my voice, or to the world around me, music would always exist for me because it was something that ran through my blood. I couldn't get away even if I wanted to.

But it wasn't the prison sentence or the curse I had thought it was. It was very much a gift.

That afternoon I had another revelation.

"That's right," Julie said, "keep breathing just like that. Those deep breaths help to center you. When you sit up straight and let your shoulders fall gently backward, you're able to open up your ribcage and take in more air. The bigger the breaths you can inhale and exhale, the more relaxed your body will be. You want to think of your center of gravity as being in your lower belly. Where did your center of gravity feel like when you were walking around just now?"

"Um, my chest?" I said, laughing a little.

"Yep, you got it. But you want your center, your core, to be where your power comes from. And your breath-work fuels that power."

"That's like singing," I said, taking in a deep, cleansing breath that I felt all the way down to my toes.

"Is it?" Julie asked. "Well, that's interesting."

"Yes, the breathwork and the chest position, too."

"I don't doubt it. Bree says that it's the same way when she does Tai Chi.

"If you watch her, you'll see that she is an excellent example of someone who uses breathwork to control her horse's pace and energy level. I don't even think she knows that she's doing it half the time, but you've probably noticed how well Nipper responds to her. She has the gift of accomplishing a lot while doing very little with her body."

"Yeah, I don't think I have that skill," I said, smiling slightly.

"Well, how long did it take you to be such a talented singer?" Julie asked, watching me curiously.

"I started singing before I could talk," I said slowly. "I don't remember anything in my life before music. It's so much a part of me now."

"Well, horses are like that for some people, too. But the rest of us have to work at it our whole lives, I'm afraid."

I nodded, thinking of the posture I used when I was practicing, how I would stand balanced with my knees slightly bent and my breathing even and my chest open, everything relaxed but charged with energy.

"Whatever you're doing, keep doing it," Julie said approvingly.

The quality of Ace's walk changed ever so slightly. His neck arched and I could feel his weight shifting backward so that it felt like we were walking uphill.

"Good girl," Julie said, "just keep breathing."

We walked around like that for a few more minutes until I was grinning from ear to ear. I imagined that I was riding a proud war horse into battle. Ace felt sturdy and powerful beneath me.

"Great, now let's try that trot again."

It still wasn't perfect. But I'd been working hard to follow Julie's instructions. I still felt awkward sometimes and like I was bouncing around too much, but Ace had an easy, steady trot. And I completely trusted him not to dump me on the ground when I was off-balance.

By the time we were done, I was exhausted but exhilarated too, and I couldn't stop petting Ace's silky neck and thanking him and Julie over and over.

I looked over anxiously to where Bree was sitting on Nipper to see what she thought.

She'd been generous to lend me Ace and I wanted to always ride my best on him. I didn't want her to ever regret her decision.

"Looking good," she said smiling, "you two work really well together."

I walked Ace around on a loose rein to cool him out, glancing down at my phone to check the time. My family, or at least part of my family, would be here in less than two hours. The thought made me excited but scared, too. All of our lives were about to be so different.

I watched as Julie moved over to Bree to give her some pointers with Nipper.

It was amazing how hard that horse worked for Bree. Julie was helping to teach her some sort of sideways movement that was somehow different than the other sideways movements they'd been working on. But whatever they were doing, it looked really polished and beautiful with Bree sitting tall and balanced and Nipper flexing his powerful neck as he floated down the long side of the ring.

I'd really had no goals when I'd come here except to escape the mortifying end of my career, but now I wondered if I could ever learn to ride like that. To look like I was fused solidly to my horse like a warrior.

I reached down and petted Ace's neck, wondering what the rest of the year was going to bring.

CHAPTER 28

ADIE

"They're here," Grady said, throwing me a suddenly panicked look as the sound of tires crunched up the driveway.

Although everyone was thrilled that he was alive and well, he was still in a lot of trouble for running away in the first place. If I knew my parents, he wasn't going to get off the hook completely.

"It's okay," I said, "they're going to be glad to see you first. The lecture and the grounding will come later."

We ran to the window to see an older blue minivan crawling its way toward the house. That was my mom all right. She always drove as if she were ninety years old.

The van opened and the twins leapt out, closely followed by Flora.

Wow, they've grown so much in such a short time, I thought, feeling a pang that I'd missed such a big chunk of their lives. Flora had her long blonde hair flying loose in the wind, getting tangled, like always. But Ivy and Izzy had both had their hair cut to shoulder-length and were wearing headbands. Which was shocking because none of us ever, ever, cut our hair. It was part of our brand.

"Come on," I said, pulling Grady with me to the front door.

Flora screamed as soon as she caught sight of us and barreled at us full-tilt, not stopping until she'd collided with us, sobbing hysterically.

"I missed you," she howled. "Grady, you shouldn't have left me like that. The twins hate me."

She kept crying while I hoisted her up and carried her into the house. And she didn't stop when I set her carefully down on the couch in the living room.

"The twins don't hate you," I said, "they just have each other so it's hard for them to remember that there are other people to play with, too. Look, here's Tom coming to say hi to you."

Flora looked up, sniffling, and stopped abruptly when she caught sight of Tom making his way slowly toward her. He jumped up on the couch and plopped himself down on her lap, purring loudly.

"He loves me," she said, her tears instantly vanishing.

"Yep, we all do. You're a lovable kid. Stay right there, I'm going to get everyone else."

I quickly went outside to where Grady was reuniting with Mom and the girls. But there was no sign of anyone else.

"I thought the whole family was coming," I said in confusion.

"Well, they are, but not right now," mom said tiredly. "Let's go inside and I'll explain."

"We're moving back home, aren't we?" Grady said excitedly, looking at her face in anticipation. "Finally. We're going back to the farm."

"Yes," Mom said. "Adie, I would love a cup of tea if you wouldn't mind. I'm exhausted from the trip"

I hurriedly made tea and brought the younger kid's cookies and juice, wishing mom could just get to the point without stalling. I wanted to know what had happened with Hope and Phil. And where my dad, Micah, and Mariam were.

"I'm taking Grady and the girls back to the farm for the summer," Mom said finally. "And we'll probably stay there next year, too. We're going to fix up that guest cottage to live in. That way we don't have to kick anyone out of the big house."

"Okay, but what about Dad? What about Micah and Mariam? And, well, I guess Hope?"

I didn't ask about Phil. I didn't care if he'd somehow been plunged to the bottom of the ocean.

Mom took a huge sigh and her eyes filled with tears for just a second.

"Your father and the older kids decided to keep on with the tour. Micah has taken over the bookings and they rewrote the music so they could use it for just the three of them. It won't be the same, of course, but it's what they all want. They want to at least make a go of it."

Wow, I sat there in disbelief, wondering how things had changed so much in such a short time.

"It's not what I would have chosen," Mom said unhappily, "but it's what your father decided to do. Micah and Mariam will be happy. But life on the road is not good for the kids. The rest of us will go back to the farm and see what happens from there."

She smiled, reached out and pulled Grady to her, managing to sneak a kiss on the top of his head before he wriggled away.

"Hope and Phil have gone their own way. We decided not to press charges, of course, but they are no longer welcome in our family. Hope says they'll be getting married next year. And we wish them the best."

Ewww, I thought, but said nothing. With any luck, I'd never have to see either of them again. But I would certainly never wish Hope the *best* of anything. I'd leave the forgiving up to Mom.

CHAPTER 29

BREE

*A*die's family stayed for a few more days and so did Angelika. Between them as houseguests, and Nicholas coming home from school after his exams, we had a completely full house.

I was surprised at how much I liked the chaos.

Everywhere I turned, someone was laughing or singing at the top of their lungs, and Ace, Bear, and Nipper were kept terribly busy giving non-stop pony rides to the kids.

Jeremy wasn't quite so thrilled with all the noise. He wasn't a fan of children it turned out, so he kept away as much as he could, eating all his meals at Lorne's house and avoiding us whenever we were in the barn.

Something which pleased Chloe to no end.

It was fascinating to hear them all working on Flora's song. She'd graciously allowed her sisters to help them with the production and all of them had hung on Angelika's every word as she coached them on how to put all the pieces together just right.

They'd practiced non-stop and then, on their final day there, they'd roped me into filming their performance.

They'd decided to do it down at the barn with the big doors rolled back so that you could see the field and the horses behind them. The barn acoustics were apparently just what they wanted. And the little girls could hardly contain themselves when they were finally ready to film it.

"This is a new song that my friends here wrote," Angelika said directly into the camera. "It's still a little rough around the edges. But right now, it sounds a little like this."

Adie played guitar and the rest of them sang and it was pretty much the most beautiful thing I'd ever heard.

I held my breath to keep the camera as still as I could but I couldn't help my hands from shaking a little.

Adie actually reminds me a bit of Angelika when she was young, I thought, feeling a pang of guilt. Never had I thrown myself into helping Angelika with her songs. We never collaborated on any type of project together. How much different would life have been for us if I'd been willing to put my jealousy aside and help her? Even just a little bit.

Everyone clapped loudly when it was over. Adie's mom had tears in her eyes, and she hugged everyone in turn, including Angelika.

I'd half-thought that Adie might decide to go home with them at the last minute. And I was ridiculously happy when she'd told me that she was planning to stay on with us.

I'd grown to love her like a sister, and I couldn't imagine not having her here and sharing Ace with her.

That night, the house seemed much quieter once everyone had left. But it had a peaceful feel to it, too.

Nicholas and I sat on the couch late into the night, half-watching a movie and half-talking excitedly about our plans for the future. I had a horse show to plan for the end of the summer and Nicholas was dead set on us taking some sort of adventure vacation together.

It would have to be close to home since neither of us really had any money to travel, but I was up for anything. Even camping didn't sound so horrifying if it meant spending time together. Right then, anything felt possible when he was beside me.

CHAPTER 30

BREE

*W*e managed to go an entire couple of weeks before the next drama hit us. And this time, Chloe was the cause of it.

"I've decided," she told me, "I don't care what my parents say. I'm coming to live here for the summer. I don't want to miss out on any more time with Dragon. And I just know that Jeremy is going to try and convince Lorne to let him ride her if I'm not around."

She wasn't completely off-base about that. It was no secret that Jeremy admired Dragon and he'd mentioned a couple of times how he'd like to start riding her.

"Great," I'd told her excitedly, "you can have the room next to mine. I can't wait."

A few days later, I found Chloe in the barn, brushing Dragon despondently.

"So, how did it go?" I asked tentatively, noticing her tense shoulders and the jerky movements that she used to run the brush over Dragon's neck.

Normally, the big horse might have made faces at such careless treatment, but for some reason she was being extra tolerant. She turned to nuzzle Chloe's arm and snorted.

Chloe didn't say anything for a few seconds. I heard her sigh heavily and then sniff.

"It was about as bad as I expected." She dropped the brush in the nearby grooming box and turned to face me, leaning her back against Dragon's shoulder a little for support.

"She won't let you come?"

"Oh, I'm coming. She didn't have much choice. It's not like she can stop me. But she certainly didn't make it easy on me."

"She was mad?"

"Livid. I don't think I've ever seen her so angry. My brothers pretty much just fled to their rooms and hid. She called my dad and raged at him, saying he'd turned me against her. And then she …"

Chloe hesitated, her forehead wrinkling unhappily. "She sort of kicked me out, actually."

"Kicked you out? But you were planning to move out anyway."

"Yeah, but she told me to take all my stuff by the weekend and that I'm not welcome back."

"No," I said in astonishment. As crazy as my own mother could be, I couldn't imagine her ever doing such a thing.

Chloe's face crumpled and she turned back to face Dragon, pressing her forehead into the big mare's mane.

"Chloe, that is awful. I'm so sorry."

"She said that I had until the weekend to get all my things and then she's giving everything else away to charity. I don't even know how I'm supposed to fit everything into my car. I mean, like, how do you move a bed and dresser? And where am I going to put them anyway?"

"Don't worry about that. I'm sure we can store your stuff here for now. And we can take Lorne's and Julie's cars, too. We'll all go together."

"Oh, you don't have to do that," Chloe said quickly. "She'll be really mad if lots of people show up and I don't want anyone else to get yelled at."

"So, who cares if she yells? You're part of a team here, Chloe. So, if one of us gets yelled at, we all get yelled at."

She snorted with laughter and wiped her eyes. "Thanks, Bree. Yeah, okay, that would be great. Maybe we can go on Friday when she's hopefully at work. I still have my key if she hasn't already changed all the locks."

"I'm sure she wouldn't do that …" I started to say but Chloe's dark look had me trailing off. Her mom did sound pretty intense at the moment. "Well, let's figure it out tonight at dinner when everyone is around."

Lorne and Julie were thoroughly outraged when she'd told the whole story again that night over dessert. We had to calm Lorne down several times or he probably would have driven to Chloe's house right there and then if we hadn't had overruled him.

Once we calmed him down, he got very quiet and just meditatively sipped his drink while the rest of us talked. I didn't think he'd let it go, though; he had the aura of someone who was plotting something on his own.

He left shortly after that without hanging out in front of the woodstove like he usually did when he came for dinner. Julie watched him leave with her eyes narrowed, clearly sharing my suspicions that he was up to something.

The next morning, we had our answer. I heard the rumble of a truck coming up the driveway. It was barely even light out and I looked out my bedroom window to see who on earth would be coming to see us this early.

To my surprise, it was an older blue truck pulling a shiny white horse trailer and instead of going to the barn it pulled up to Lorne's little cabin and shuddered to a stop. A younger man hopped out and I could see Lorne meet him at the front door and usher him inside.

Curious, I hurriedly dressed and made my way downstairs and put on my outdoor gear. I would feed the horses an early breakfast and just stop in at Lorne's on the way down.

But by the time I got outside and was walking down the hill, the man had come back outside, hopped in Lorne's old car, backed it out the driveway and sped away.

Okay, now I really want to know what's happening, I thought, picking up the pace.

Lorne met me outside with a grin on his face.

"Well, you're up early," he said, not looking at all surprised to see me.

"Did you buy this?" I asked incredulously. He'd been holding out on getting a horse trailer until we really needed one and I'd pretty much thought he'd put it off forever.

"Might have," he said, winking at me. "What do you think of it?"

"I love it." I walked around the truck and trailer, admiring them from all angles. "Chloe is going to be so excited. She's wanted to start taking Dragon out for like forever. And, oh, we can use it to help her move."

"Yes, what a coincidence." Lorne squeezed my shoulder and gave me a little push toward the barn. "Now, we have to make this trailer earn its keep. I expect to see you out performing at some shows, missy. Now, go feed those critters. I think I'm going to get another cup of coffee."

CHAPTER 31

BREE

$\mathcal{I}$t turned out that moving Chloe out of her house wasn't as traumatic as we'd expected. Nobody was home when we showed up with the truck and trailer. Chloe's mother had already stuffed her clothes and things into boxes and had them stacked by the front door. And the bed and dresser were easy enough to get down the stairs.

Chloe cried a little anyway, probably more from nerves than anything else, but she cheered up once we were back at the farm.

And, mostly to distract her, Lorne announced that night that he'd signed us all up for our first show. Even Adie, to her utter astonishment.

"It's just a little schooling show," Lorne said, waving his hand in the air dismissively. "And it's all on the flat so you shouldn't embarrass yourselves too much."

It turned out that it was a casual dressage show put on by the local club. We didn't even have to get dressed up in show clothes if we didn't want to. Which was perfect because I didn't own any and neither did Adie.

Adie and I were both riding Ace in different tests. Hers was a walk-trot test that Ace could do in his sleep as long as the excitement of the show grounds didn't get to him. And I was taking both him and Nipper in a couple of Training level tests.

Chloe was taking both Dragon and Nugget, and Jeremy was to enter Timely and Rabbit.

"It's really just a chance to see how they all behave off property," Julie said when I confessed that I was nervous. "We need an idea of what each horse needs to work on so we don't have any surprises when we really start showing. Don't worry about your test scores at all this time. It's just for fun and experience."

There were so many of us going that we had to trailer the horses over in shifts, and the air was thick with excitement. I was pretty sure the racehorses thought they were headed back to the track because they were all on their toes and bellowing the second it was time to load them in the trailer.

We hadn't braided anyone, but their manes were pulled short and neatly brushed. Each horse had had a bath and were looking as well as could be expected without having completely shed out.

Our tack was clean. Our riding clothes were neat, and Julie had given Adie and I matching black fitted vests to wear.

Chloe and Jeremy had actual show coats, and I couldn't help but be envious over how well turned out and professional they looked.

Our horses weren't exactly the best-behaved group when we first arrived at the show grounds. We'd made sure to get there early which was good because it took them a long time to settle down.

For the first half-hour, it was just non-stop neighing and pacing. I saw some of the other competitors look at our horses wide-eyed as they passed by. I was glad we hadn't had a chance to put the farm logo on the trailer yet.

Whose idea had it been to bring a whole pack of baby horses to this show anyway?

Finally, at some point, our horses must have realized that there wasn't a racetrack anywhere in sight. First one, and then another started eating their hay and gradually the energy levels dropped, and they were able to look around the show grounds with interest.

Eventually, we were able to take a couple up at a time and either lead or hack them around the grounds so they could stretch their legs and do a bit of a warm-up.

Ace had settled down really well. He was actually calmer than Nipper was.

Because of the way the show schedule was laid out, Adie had to ride him in her test first. Something which made me anxious. But she'd said no when I'd offered to warm him up for her and had quietly walked and trotted him around the warm-up ring without a problem.

Her test went just fine. They had just walked and trotted around sedately and didn't make any huge mistakes. I had no idea what the judge thought, but I was incredibly proud of her. Of both of them.

"You ready for this?" Nicholas said, resting his hand lightly on my leg as he leaned over to adjust the twist in Ace's reins.

I smiled down at him and nodded, then reached out and ran a hand quickly through his hair where the wind had blown it in all directions. I pulled back right away, half-embarrassed about manhandling him in public, but he only laughed.

"You sure you don't want me to read your test for you?"

"Nope," I shook my head and smiled. "Ace and I have got this."

The rider ahead of me walked out of the ring on a loose rein. She patted her horse automatically on the neck, but her expression was grim. I hadn't been paying attention to her at all, but I suspected that things hadn't gone well.

"All right, buddy," I told Ace. "We're up. Let's go have some fun."

And that's what we did. Yes, he moved along at a glacial pace like he was about to stop and have a nap at any moment. And it was true that he didn't have half the presence and charisma that Nipper carried with him into the ring. But he trundled happily along, not caring that it was his first show or that there was a crowd of people. Just steadily, kindly doing what I asked him to do and no more.

And really, wasn't that enough to expect of him?

When it was over, I was prouder of him than I'd ever been of anyone. I leaned down and hugged him hard around the neck.

The rest of the show went pretty much the way we'd expected. Timely behaved like a professional gentleman and the judge waved Jeremy over at the end so he could tell him what a nice horse he had.

Dragon jumped out of the ring and took off through the showgrounds, nearly bucking Chloe off.

Nugget was calm and actually came away with a pretty good test score for his first show ever. Rabbit travelled along with his nose in the air the whole time, but he kept his cool and didn't do anything too silly.

And Nipper pranced his way through his entire test, showing his flashing gaits off and arching his neck like he'd been waiting for just that moment to show himself off to the world.

"Oh, my gosh, Bree, that was fantastic," Julie said, coming over to hug us both. But all the credit went to Nipper. I'd just told him where to go, he'd thrown in all the fancy stuff on his own.

I came away with a fourth and a sixth-place ribbon, which was kind of incredible since I still felt like I barely knew what I was doing.

All in all, it had been a pretty amazing start to the season. The horses would gain experience and we would, too. The summer was just going to get better and better.

That night I proudly hung my ribbons up on my bedroom mirror where I could look at them as I fell asleep.

CHAPTER 32

BREE

"*S*omebody wants to come and look at Rabbit," Julie announced the next week at the breakfast table.

"He's not ready," Jeremy said without looking up. "And we're not selling to anyone who wants to jump him."

Julie sent him a dark look and cleared her throat. "Anyway, as I was *saying*, she's actually the student of an old friend of mine. She's a dressage rider. And she saw Rabbit at the show. She wants to try him."

"But he's still really green," Chloe said, frowning. "I thought we weren't adopting them out while they were still green."

"Yes, normally, I'd agree with you. But her coach, Claudia, is amazing with the green horses. I've known her for years and I trust her judgement. She called me last night and said that she thinks Rabbit might be a match for this student she has. I couldn't say no."

"Well, let's have her out here," Lorne said, rubbing his hands together. "If he goes off to a new home, I'll call Eddie to see about sending us another horse."

"Let's not get ahead of ourselves," Julie warned. "It might not work out."

But later that day, we all managed to be at the barn doing odd chores when the prospective new owner and her coach showed up.

"She's fat," Jeremy said flatly, narrowing his eyes at the two women who were emerging out of the shiny black SUV.

They were both wearing breeches and boots. One of them was tall and willowy and carried herself with the regal carriage of a dancer. The other one looked a little more like I probably would when I was middle-aged. Her shirt was half-untucked and her hair was coming out of its ponytail. You could see the green smudge on her breeches from here. And, yeah, she was a little overweight. So what. She looked kind and that was what was going to matter to Rabbit.

"Stop body shaming," Chloe said, turning to look at Jeremy over her shoulder with disgust. "She looks a little out of shape, that's all. It's not like she'll be too heavy for him or anything. He's built like a tank."

"He needs a fit rider. He'll get all strung out if she's not balanced. She looks disorganized. I hate a disorganized woman."

Chloe, her eyes flashing, opened her mouth to say something scathing.

"Well, how about we not have this conversation right now?" Julie said, appearing behind us. She looked meaningfully at Jeremy until he glanced away, concentrating on running the soft brush over Rabbit's glistening neck. "And please be polite."

She put on her most charming smile and then went to meet the two ladies who were now standing in the barn doorway.

"Claudia," Julie called, a note of genuine happiness in her voice.

To my surprise, she and the willowy lady shared a long hug and when they broke away, they both had tears in their eyes.

"It's been much too long, my friend," the coach, Claudia, said. "I've missed you. I'm sorry, this is one of my favourite students, Pender. Pender, this is my old friend, Julie."

"Hello," Julie said, wiping her eyes a little and laughing despite her tears, "sorry, Pender, you must think we're the silliest things to be crying over nothing. Let's go meet this horse."

"Ooh, he's big," the woman, Pender, said, eyeing Rabbit up with shining eyes. "Could I give him a carrot?"

Rabbit's big ears shot forward and his eyes gleamed as he locked his gaze on the carrot piece she was pulling out of her pocket. His upper lip twitched back and forth in anticipation.

"He doesn't need treats," Jeremy snapped, pressing his mouth into a thin line and making Rabbit back up sharply a few steps to discourage him. "He'll get pushy if he's hand fed. And fat."

"Of course, he can have a carrot," Julie said at the same time. "Jeremy, I think we've got it from here. Thanks for your help, though. I think Lorne was hoping you'd help him up at his house."

Jeremy gave her an angry look and muttered something under his breath as he marched away.

Pender watched him go with wide eyes, the carrot piece still clutched in her outstretched hand.

"Oh, don't mind him," Julie said quickly. "He's a bit of a work in progress. Moody but a hard worker."

"Okay," Pender said uncertainly.

There was a moment of silence, which Rabbit abruptly ended when he surged forward and took the carrot firmly out of Pender's hand and began to crunch it greedily.

That broke the tension completely and everyone started to laugh.

"Chloe, do you mind getting his tack? I was going to have

Jeremy ride him for us, but maybe you don't mind doing it instead?"

"No problem," Chloe said, sending Pender a reassuring smile. "He's really friendly. He's like a big dog and wants to be in your pocket all the time."

Pender was smiling dreamily now as she stood at Rabbit's big shoulder and ran her hand down his neck. He turned his head toward her as far as the cross-ties would allow and nuzzled her arm gently.

"He does have a few quirks in the barn," Julie told them. "Like I mentioned on the phone. But he's great under saddle and he's an all-around good guy. We've only shown him the one time, but he's great to trailer and I think he did pretty well for his first show."

"Oh, I saw his test. I thought he did really well for a young horse," Pender said. "Besides, I don't plan to show much. I mostly like to study dressage at home. Riding is my escape from being a full-time mom in a house full of boys."

"Well, this guy sure likes to be pampered. We've taken him on the trail, and he's been excellent in company, although he does get nervous when he's alone."

"Oh, I don't like riding out alone," Pender said quickly. "But I do like to go on the trails with some of the other ladies at the barn at least once a week. We have some bridges and water to cross. Would he do that?"

"Yep, absolutely. Jeremy has ridden him through all sorts of terrain. He's a brave horse as long as he's not alone."

"Well, that's sounds nice."

Everyone stepped back a little to watch while Chloe tacked Rabbit up.

For once, Rabbit stood rock-still, not pawing or tossing his head or pulling back in the cross-ties. He was on his best-behaviour, which I thought was maybe a little misleading for these people.

He stayed perfectly at Chloe's shoulder without barging ahead or trying to pull, and I noticed that he was keeping a close eye on Pender. He was probably still thinking about that carrot.

"I don't often ride him," Chloe said, tightening the girth and swinging up on him from the mounting block. "It might take me a few minutes to get used to him."

She moved him off at a walk, letting him stride across the ring on a loose rein, his head bobbing and his body swaying.

"You can see how much he overtracks," Julie said, laughing a little. "He really is like a baby dinosaur and we think he's still growing even though he's five. He's clumsy sometimes but so honest. Jeremy really likes him."

Claudia and Pender nodded but said nothing. Claudia was watching him with her eyes narrowed and Pender had her hands clasped under her chin and an excited smile on her face like a kid about to open a birthday present.

Chloe let him walk around the ring for a few minutes, doing circles and serpentines to loosen him up. Then she shortened her reins a little and let him leap up into his ground covering trot.

"Wow," Pender said, "I love him."

Claudia smiled and patted her friend on the arm.

"That's what you say about all of them. But, I have to admit that I like him, too."

"His canter needs some work," Julie warned, "he's still all over the place. He's much more balanced on the trails than in the ring. He's got such a big stride that I think he feels a little confined cantering in here."

Chloe let him lumber around the outside of the ring with his big, goofy stride that nearly took him from one end to the other in one bound.

"Yes," Claudia said, suppressing a smile. "I see what you mean. He needs to grow into those legs. He certainly doesn't seem bothered by anything, though."

"Well, he does have his baby moments from time to time,"

Julie warned, "but he's an overall good egg. Do you want to try him?"

"Yes," Pender breathed, her face glowing with excitement. "I do."

She sounded like she was completely in love already.

She looked a little more nervous when he was standing beside the mounting block and she was about to climb on, though. He was a lot of horse when you were standing on the ground beside him.

"Don't worry," Claudia said reassuringly. "Just walk him around and get a feel for him. No pressure."

"Okay," Pender said, taking a deep breath and then climbing nimbly into the saddle. She sat there for a moment, nosing her feet into the stirrups and quietly petting Rabbit's neck.

"Right, walk on fellow," she said, gathering her reins.

He flicked his ears back at her uncertainly, not certain about this new rider but after a second he moved forward around the ring, gaining speed and confidence as he went.

"Good boy," Pender said, relaxing in her seat. A smile playing around her mouth.

She didn't look disorganized or awkward at all in the saddle. You could tell that she was in her element on a horse.

She took him around the outside of the ring a few times and then began moving him in circles and figures and even triangles around the ring. He strode along, marching with his ears pricked and his mouth lightly working at the bit. A layer of light foam coated his lips.

"How does he feel?" Claudia called.

"Great, actually. I'm going to trot him."

"Sure, go for it," Claudia said, raising her eyebrows. I had the feeling that maybe Pender wasn't the bravest of riders normally.

Pender shortened her reins and asked the big horse to move on.

She made a slight squeaking noise as he leapt up into his trot and she was thrown back a little in the saddle. But it only took a second for her to recover before she moved back into sync with him.

She was light and balanced and her position was solid.

Rabbit stretched his neck down and out, bringing his back up and swinging with his hindquarters.

Claudia began to smile, and she nodded her head a few times as if confirming something to herself.

Pender rode him for another fifteen minutes, not saying a word, just trotting him in big loops and spirals with a big smile on her face.

She brought him down to a walk and couldn't stop patting his neck in excitement.

"I want him," she said, grinning from ear to ear. "When can we pick him up?"

"Um, vet check? Negotiating? Playing it cool?" Claudia said, pushing back her smile and raising an eyebrow. "You are a terrible horse shopper."

"Oh, I know," Pender said gleefully. She swung down lightly to the ground and gave Rabbit a big hug around his neck. "I suppose we should get the vet check, but I already know he'll pass. And his price is fine. I don't need to negotiate. Would you like a deposit to hold him?" This last part was said to Julie.

"Oh, don't worry about that," Julie said. "You rode him beautifully. And I'm glad you like him."

"We'll set up a pre-purchase exam for this week just to be safe," Claudia said, "but I agree that this could be a very good match for you, Pender."

"I should mention that he was on his best behaviour today in the barn," Julie said. "I want to be very upfront that he has some quirks on the ground. And he can be hard to catch sometimes. I don't want you to be surprised when you get him home."

"I'm sure," Pender said happily. "One hundred percent."

We were all grinning from ear to ear. Pender spent nearly an hour grooming Rabbit after their ride and her coach finally had to drag her away.

The vet exam was booked for a few days' time, and everyone was thrilled about our first sale except, of course, Jeremy.

He wasn't quite as bad about it as he'd been earlier. Despite being banished back to Lorne's house, he'd sneakily watched Pender do her test-ride from the hill above the barn. Even he had to admit that she'd ridden him well.

"So maybe it's not the worst home," he admitted over dinner, where we'd gathered to celebrate. "Even if she is a bit of a mess. I'll miss him, though. He's a good boy. Even if he can't jump."

Julie narrowed her eyes at Jeremy, and I knew she was remembering how rude he'd been to Pender. That had been an unpleasant window into his character. And I wondered how much longer Julie was going to tolerate having him around. I had the feeling that his days at the farm were numbered.

The kitchen table was loaded with food and nearly every chair was full. Nicholas was home for the weekend and I'd already roped him into the promise of a real trail ride.

"Well, now we are really and truly on our way," Lorne said, loudly popping the cork on the bottle of champagne he'd brought. "Our first show and our first sale. The future is truly looking bright. Gretta would be so proud."

"She absolutely would be," Julie agreed, reaching over to squeeze his hand.

And as I looked around the table at the people I loved best in the world, I had to agree.

Later that night, Adie, Chloe, and I meandered our way down to the barn together to do one last check on the horses.

The stars overhead had come out full-force in the cloudless sky, looking like they'd been painted there by some master artist.

I tilted my head way back and studied them as I walked, a

deep contentment filling me right to my very bones. I had never felt so strongly alive as I did right then.

The horses nickered sleepily as Chloe rolled back the outer door and flicked on the light.

"Sorry to wake you all up," Adie said, going straight to Ace's stall. She peered in and smiled, waving me over.

"He's sleeping," she said in a whisper and we peered in to see Ace stretched right out on his side, snoring heavily, his eyes and nose twitching a little as if he were in the middle of a dream.

"That means that they're happy and relaxed when they sleep like that," Chloe said, "it means that they feel comfortable enough to let down their guard and not worry about predators. He knows he's safe here and that nothing will hurt him."

There was a soft thumping noise and we looked up to see Dragon standing at the edge of her stall, staring at Chloe, her ears swiveling and her eyes bright and alert.

"Unlike someone we know," I said with a laugh. "I don't think she'll ever let her guard down."

"Maybe not," Chloe said, fishing a carrot out of her pocket and walking over to the big mare. Dragon stood politely, not pinning her ears at all, and lipped the carrot gently out of Chloe's hand. "But that's because she's a born leader. That's what makes her special."

I shook my head and smiled and the two of them. Dragon had finished her carrot and had moved on to checking out Chloe's many pockets one by one.

"Hey, Chill-Chill," Chloe said, moving over to Chilly's stall and smiling in at him. He was lying down too, his head up and his legs tucked neatly under his body. She rolled back his door and went slowly inside, not stopping until she'd crouched down in the bedding near his head.

He snorted softly but didn't get up and he happily took the treat she offered him.

"Do you think he'll be all right eventually?" she asked,

glancing down at his foreleg and then reaching out and running her fingers through his mane.

I hesitated and then nodded. "Yeah, I do," I said, suddenly feeling the truth in those words. The past season had been hard for me but I felt like I'd grown, become a stronger, more resilient person. And the future was looking bright. "I think we're all going to be just fine."

The End

Stay tuned for *Keeping Chilly*, the third book in the October Horses series.

ACKNOWLEDGMENTS

This one goes out to so many people!

Thanks to Sharon Tomczyk at Esteem Vocals for the fantastic online singing lessons and for letting me pick your brain about what a musician's life is really like.

Thanks to excellent coaches and horsewomen, Gina Allan (https://ginaallan.ca/) and Jennifer Derksen, The Rider Mechanic, (http://www.theridermechanic.com/) for your amazing insights on horse psychology, biomechanics and fitness. The horses thank you too!

Big thanks to Helen Cartwright, Helen Yeo, Honey Johnston, Mariko Brown, Jules Kirby, and the rest of the fantastic Advanced Reader team. Your insights are always invaluable.

Always thankful for the current ponies in my life, Messenger and Fiona, and to all the past horses and ponies who taught me so much.

ABOUT THE AUTHOR

Genevieve McKay is the author of over a dozen books, and most of them are about horses. She is an avid reader, baker, eater of snacks and a tea-drinker. She lives on the west coast of Canada with her family, her horses, and an assortment of barnyard animals like dogs, cats, sheep, chickens and two half-tame ravens.

Visit my website at www.genevievemckay.com
Follow my pics on Instagram: @mckaygenevieve
Or join my Facebook author page: www. facebook.com/authorgenevievemckay

BOOKS AND RESOURCES

If you are enjoying the October Horses series, Defining Gravity series or any of my other books, I'd love if you'd take a moment to write a review on Amazon, Goodreads or any of the platforms where they are sold.

The October Horses series

The October Horses

Facing The Fire

Keeping Chilly (Coming soon)

Defining Gravity series

Defining Gravity

Flight

Freefall

Riding Above Air

Touching Ground

Short Stories and Collections

The Horses of Winter

Greystone Manor mystery series (under G.M. Mckay)

The Curse of the Golden Touch

The Sting of the Serpent's Blade

If you're interested in learning more about adopting a retired racehorse then here are some great resources to get you started!

The Retired Racehorse Project

https://www.retiredracehorseproject.org/

Greener Pastures

https://greenerpasturesbc.com/

Retraining of Racehorses

https://www.ror.org.uk/

And New Track, New Life is a fantastic resource to have:

New Track New Life

Visit my website at www.genevievemckay.com

Follow my pics on Instagram: @mckaygenevieve

Or join my Facebook author page: www.
facebook.com/authorgenevievemckay

Printed in Great Britain
by Amazon

48649273R00148